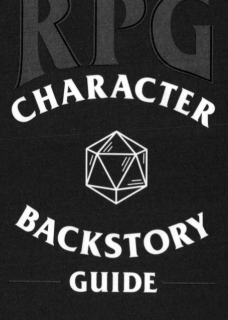

THE ULTIMATE RPG CHARACTER BACKSTORY GUIDE

PROMPTS AND ACTIVITIES TO CREATE THE MOST INTERESTING STORY FOR YOUR CHARACTER

JAMES D'AMATO

ADAMS MEDIA

NEW YORK LONDON TORONTO SYDNEY NEW DELHI

Adams Media
An Imprint of Simon & Schuster, Inc.
57 Littlefield Street
Avon, Massachusetts 02322

First Adams Media trade paperback edition October 2018

Interior design by Colleen Cunningham

Manufactured in the United States of America

10 9 8 7 6 5 4 3

Library of Congress Cataloging-in-Publication Data
D'Amato, James.
The ultimate RPG character backstory guide / James D'Amato.
Avon, Massachusetts: Adams Media, 2018.
LCCN 2018018954 | ISBN 9781507208373 (pb) | ISBN 9781507208380 (ebook)
Subjects: LCSH: Fantasy games--Handbooks, manuals, etc. | Avatars (Virtual reality)--Handbooks, manuals, etc. | BISAC: GAMES / Role Playing & Fantasy. | GAMES / General. | LANGUAGE ARTS & DISCIPLINES / Composition & Creative Writing.
Classification: LCC GV1469.6 .D36 2018 | DDC 793.93--dc23
LC record available at https://lccn.loc.gov/2018018954

ISBN 978-1-5072-0837-3
ISBN 978-1-5072-0838-0 (ebook)

Contents

Humble Beginnings...9

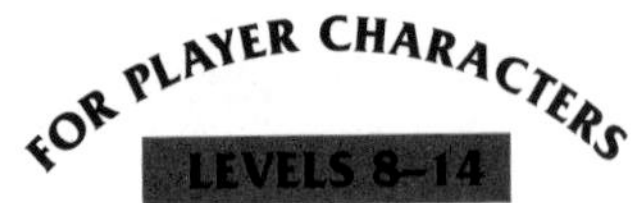

Veteran Heroes...105

Myths and Legends...197

Introduction

Sitting around a table with your friends, rolling dice and cross-checking charts, slaying monsters and looting treasure hoards, you know the fun, the creative joy, of playing role-playing games. You may have slain your first goblin while playing Dungeons & Dragons (D&D), but these days there are dozens of RPGs in a variety of settings.

Whether your player character (PC) is prowling around a moldy dungeon in search of gold or battling a crowd of orcs on a bridge that spans a bottomless abyss, a lot of the fun of RPGs comes from *how* your character reacts to any given challenge. This book will help you explore this dimension of gaming.

How your PC handles a problem depends on what shaped the character into who she or he is. In these pages you'll find exercises that will challenge you to create a richer past for the hero you've brought to life.

You can complete most of these exercises on your own. Others might be more fun to do with your gaming buddies. Some exercises are crafted with specific character types in mind. (For example, Orphan Details is geared toward characters who are orphans.) There is no particular order to these activities, and you should feel free to hop around the book to find the activities best suited to your character. To make hunting a little easier, this book is divided into three sections for low-, middle-, and high-level characters.

- **Choose your answer from the options listed**
- **Roll a six-sided die (d6), a ten-sided die (d10), or a twenty-sided die (d20) for an auto-generated answer**
- **Write your answer out**

Many of the exercises in this book will address your character as "you" the way a game master might. Whenever the book is asking about physical qualities or background details, we're talking about characters and not you, the reader. So get started! You've got a character to create and worlds to explore!

What Can We Accomplish?

With all the possibilities a fantasy world contains, you may find it difficult to determine what challenges you should take on. All too often heroes shy from challenges beneath their capability or charge headlong into situations they are not prepared for. Following is a guide that provides a rough idea of what you should be able to accomplish. It is possible for powerful characters to be unlucky and make mistakes or for weaker characters to be prudent and fortunate, but generally, this list will provide you with a starting point for your level.

LEVELS 1–5

- Survive a relatively unlucky day
- Survive an encounter with a fairly dangerous animal
- Win a bar fight
- Hunt a large nonmagical beast
- Fend off a coordinated bandit attack

LEVELS 6–10

- Compete in a gladiatorial arena
- Hold off a squad of trained soldiers
- Defeat a giant monster terrorizing a community
- Unseat a corrupt governor
- Recover an ancient and powerful secret
- Match wits with a deviously intelligent monster

LEVELS 11–15

- Become a champion in a massive competition
- Have your actions declared miraculous
- Avert a natural disaster
- Unseat a powerful tyrant

LEVELS 16–19

- Seal an ancient evil
- Battle an army with a small party
- Settle a cosmic dispute
- Destroy an interplanar threat

LEVEL 20

- Defy a god

Humble Beginnings

1 Idioms

This is a fantasy idiom generator.

2 Save the Cat

This will help you determine your character's alignment based on the level of personal risk he or she is willing to take to save a cat.

3 Holidays

In the place you grew up, there was an annual celebration that stuck with you. No matter where you are, you try to introduce this custom to the people you are with. This uses random tables and fill-in-the-blanks to create a wild holiday and determine how people react to it.

4 What Gets Left Behind

In setting out to adventure, your character abandoned things. These bittersweet prompts will create objects that your character put down, never to touch again.

5 Beanstalk

Through foolishness, carelessness, weakness, or some combination of the three, your character has lost your party's fortune to a swindler. This will help readers form a picture of how their characters react to an unavoidable social crisis.

6 Five Lessons

Your character learned five lessons he or she carries on the road and into dungeons. Some have saved his or her life; others have put him or her in danger; all of them make your character a hero. This provides a framework for ideology and behavior.

7 Ventur

Picture an app that helps adventuring parties find one another. This is a list of hero profiles. Whom do you swipe right?

8 My Associates

An inventory of surface-level thoughts about the group your character travels with. Questions that will guide readers to think about the other characters at their table.

9 Across a Crowded Tavern

Inns tend to have at least one cloaked figure seated in a dark corner looking to offer a job to the right heroes. What would one of these people notice about your character?

10 Orphan Details

Many heroes are motivated by tragedy, but without compelling details, those stories tend to run together. This exercise helps readers add evocative detail to clichéd tragic backstories.

11 What Can You Do for Me?

A guide to defining what your character wants from his or her companions.

12 A Matter of Status

Learn the concept of status within a scene and how you can move it about. Create modifiers to help people abstract your character's social status.

13 What Drives You Forward?

An exercise to help develop the ways in which your core motivations spur your decisions.

14 Where I'm From

Create a snapshot of where you came from and your life there.

15 Finders Keepers

Your character happens upon the body of a fallen adventurer. How do you handle the situation? A flowchart game that asks players to make tough moral decisions and decide what they owe a stranger.

16 Well Worn

The objects carried by heroes are tools as well as a form of self-expression. This exercise helps you further define your look by adding a wealth of small details to your equipment.

17 Five Things You Packed but Shouldn't Have

What five things does an inexperienced adventurer take with him or her?

18 Of the Cloth

Charts to help players visualize different ways to play a character whose religion is a major theme.

19 Five Fears

At this point in your career you are vulnerable and know little of the world. What fears has that led you to carry?

29 Familiar, but Not Too Familiar

Familiars and animal companions all too often get left out of the game. This exercise will add quirks and personality to your animal friends to give them a shot at longevity.

30 A Touch of Home

Staying at inns can feel exhausting. What do you do to make strange rooms feel like yours?

31 Vision of the Future

You are visited by a version of yourself from the future. Prompts for humorous self-reflection.

32 Mentor

Create a mentor for your character: reputation, relationship, resources, skills, accessibility. Assign priorities.

33 Magic Mirrors

One of the most insidious magical devices is the magic mirror. It whispers lies and truths that beguile heroes and lead them astray. What will it try to tell you?

34 Visualizing Intellect

There is more than one flavor of smart character. Creating a visual guide to your approach to intelligence can help you diversify your playstyle and keep characters feeling fresh even when they have the same stats.

Idioms

A great way to make a world feel lived in is to find a unique way for your character to speak. Idioms are a perfect new way to communicate without totally reinventing language. Roll a d6 for details and pick appropriate connecting words to create commonsense phrases that exist in a world unlike our own. Then work the phrases into your character's everyday conversation.

Choose one of the following words or roll on the profession or monster table to start your idiom:

YOU/MAGIC/GOLD/BLOOD	
1	can't find...
2	shouldn't count...
3	spent...
4	might lose...
5	won't...
6	can't make...

A RAGING.../PLEASE A.../ON A.../A FOOLISH.../A.../...

	Professions		Monsters		Riches
1	Wizard	1	Dragon	1	Gold
2	King	2	Vampire	2	Blood
3	Princess	3	Owlbear	3	Faith
4	Jester	4	Observer	4	Happiness
5	Thief	5	Mind Tyrant	5	Love
6	Peasant	6	Mimic	6	Health

continued

.../WITHOUT.../FOR.../ENDS WITH.../IN...	
Conditions	**Actions**
1 with a dwarf	1 digging a grave
2 over a barrel	2 swinging a sword
3 with one arm	3 holding your nose
4 dancing alone	4 tilling a field
5 trusting a stranger	5 lugging a pack
6 between the sheets	6 climbing a mountain
Results	**Places**
1 getting you killed	1 a river to drink
2 getting you paid	2 the deepest mine
3 suffering a god	3 the darkest dungeon
4 going broke	4 an aging castle
5 losing your way	5 under the stars
6 finding a dragon's horde	6 hell's black gates

Save the Cat

Alignment can be tricky. Saying a character is good, evil, or neutral leaves so much undefined. This chart will help you navigate those shades of gray based on what your character would be willing to do for a cat stuck in a tree.

Choose where your character might fall based on what he or she would or would not do:

Evil Actions	Set the tree on fire.	Throw a rock at the cat.
Save the cat and use the story to get elected to a political office that will allow you to close the city's animal shelters, forcing thousands of feral cats to take residence in trees.	Bind the cat's spirit to the tree, making it a vengeful guardian of the very tree that imprisoned it.	Build a series of deadly traps around the tree to kill any potential rescuers.
Use magic to conceal the tree so the cat never gets rescued.	Convince a child to save the cat, injuring both in the process.	Grumpily wonder if anyone would rescue you if you got stuck in a tree.

continued

Neutral Actions	Feel guilty that you don't have time to help the cat.	Wonder aloud, "Hey, whose cat?"
Say, "Hey, cat! Get down here!" Shrug. Walk away.	Defensively justify to the cat why you can't save it right now as it watches you with anxious disinterest.	Sit watching the cat until it gets down safely on its own. Feel relieved that everything worked out okay.

Good Actions	Find a ladder to rescue the cat.	Rescue the cat.
Rescue the cat. Form a deep emotional bond with it as you nurse it back to health. Adopt it.	Battle the horde of undead terrors who chased the cat into the tree.	Evade the wild dogs that chased the cat into the tree. Rescue the cat.
Evade the wild dogs that chased the cat into the tree. Rescue the cat. Train the wild dogs to be emotional support animals.		Free-climb forty feet into a thorny tree to rescue the cat.

Holidays

Where you come from, people celebrate a holiday not observed in other parts of the world. The coming of that day reminds you of home, but it is also something of an obligation. This exercise will help you create the structure of an unusual holiday you celebrate.

Roll a d6 four times:

This day celebrates:	With:
1 Something you should actually be ashamed of	1 A feast
2 Fertility	2 A dance
3 The poor	3 Fasting
4 A fallen hero	4 A sacrifice
5 A great kindness	5 A contest
6 The harvest	6 An intimate ceremony

But:
1 It takes materials expensive in this region.
2 You need your whole party to do it right.
3 People have to dress a particular way.
4 You have to hunt a specific beast.
5 It requires a mating ritual.
6 Everyone must tell a story.

And if you don't celebrate:
1 You won't be respected as an adult.
2 You will be considered a blasphemer.
3 You will be cursed with bad luck.
4 You will sink into a depression.
5 You won't be able to look your parent in the eye.
6 You will be overcome with supernatural rage.

This holiday is called _______________.

It is... (check all that apply)

- O Cultural
- O Civic
- O Religious
- O Enforced magically

Write your companions' names in the roles for celebrating the holiday, roles you think they would be best suited for:

_______________ would be perfect to help prepare decorations because of his, her, or their eye for detail.

_______________ has the voice of an angel and must sing.

There is no better partner than _______________ for the most difficult task before me.

I will tell _______________ first because he, she, or they will best understand my need for this.

I cannot do this without _______________'s strong arms.

This must be a surprise to _______________, or everything will be ruined.

4 What Gets Left Behind

Most people think of adventurers as being larger-than-life heroes, but all heroes come from somewhere. In this exercise, you're going to explore objects associated with a life you walked away from. Choose details that will help inspire your creativity and answer the prompts to discover the building blocks of your past.

Former Flame

This object is related to a former passion. There was once something that moved you the way wealth, glory, or righteousness moves you now.

Choose two:

- I could not take this with me on the road.
- My interest slowly waned over time until my heart had fully stolen away.
- I could hold it in my hand and feel pride.
- There were many in my life who smiled when they saw this.
- Even now, I sometimes think of it during wistful nights.
- This was crafted specifically for me with love.
- I made this with my own hands.

Once you understand what this object is, write a scene explaining where it is now. Is it collecting dust? Has it worn out from use? Has it crumbled to discarded ashes?

Broken Shackle

Before your life on the road, you suffered a persistent dread that you would end up condemned to a life of unnoticed misery. You were reminded of this fear every time you touched this object.

Roll a d6 or choose:

1. This was part of a profession you are glad to have escaped.
2. It was a way for society to punish what it did not understand.
3. Every detail whispers the dark promise of tedium.
4. Its delicate features made your strong hands feel ugly and unworthy.
5. It looked old and broken before you ever touched it and looks much the same now.
6. This was given to you by someone with love in her eyes and pride in her heart.

Write about the last moment you touched this object.

Ghostly Comfort

Even if you despised your former life, there was at least one bright spot. What purpose did this serve?

Choose one:

- It helped me sleep.
- It reminded me of those I have lost.
- It was a glimmer of beauty lost in ugliness.
- It eased my pain.

In the years since, you have tried unsuccessfully to recreate what you derived from this object. Write about the moment when you decided to discard your most recent attempt.

Beanstalk

Though parties will share many victories and successes over the course of their travels, they will also face failure. Understanding how you react to failure is an important aspect of fleshing out your character. This scenario will guide you through different possibilities in a tense situation. Select details and answer the prompts to explore a crisis you might encounter in a game.

List your party by name:

1. ....
2. ....
3. ....
4. ....
5. ....

Roll a d6. (Take one reroll if you pick yourself or land on an empty spot.) The chosen member was trusted with carrying the majority of treasure won on a recent quest. He or she lost all of it.

Based on your knowledge of the character, how did he or she lose it?

- ○ **Foolishness:** He was swindled by con artists or risked it on an uncertain gamble.
- ○ **Carelessness:** She set it down in an unsafe location or fell victim to pickpockets.
- ○ **Weakness:** They gave in to a powerful vice or was overpowered by attackers.
- ○ **Callousness:** She made a decision that prioritized her needs over the party's desires. Perhaps she used the wealth to pay a personal debt or donated it to her church.

Anger

Roll again until you have selected a new party member. (It can be you.) This character reacts with heated anger.

What form does it take?

- O Violence against people
- O Violence against objects
- O Saying unforgivable things
- O Threats

How does this play out?

What about it frightens you?

Despair

Roll again until you have selected a new party member. (It can be you.) This character reacts by sinking into despair.

What form does it take?

- O Open tears
- O Silence
- O Personal destruction
- O Voicing dark thoughts

What happens when the character reaches his, her, or their lowest point?

Who helps the character recover?

Bargaining

Roll again until you have selected a new party member. (It can be you.) She or he reacts by trying to solve a problem that cannot be solved.

What form does it take?

- O Hunting an untrackable quarry
- O Constructing a plan doomed to fail
- O Making an unnecessary sacrifice
- O Calling for cooperation before settling differences

What does the character's desperation cause her, him, or them to destroy?

When does the character realize the mistake?

Acceptance

Roll again until you have selected a new party member. (It can be you.) This character reacts better to failure than you would expect.

continued

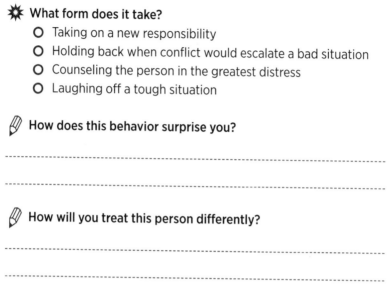

What form does it take?

- Taking on a new responsibility
- Holding back when conflict would escalate a bad situation
- Counseling the person in the greatest distress
- Laughing off a tough situation

How does this behavior surprise you?

How will you treat this person differently?

Aftermath

Once the initial shock and frustration wears off and your party is faced with the task of moving on, what makes it possible to continue together?

Choose one:

- Burying strong emotions to manifest later
- Sincere apology and strict penance
- Warm compassion and difficult forgiveness
- Reluctant belief in greater good

When does this situation next get mentioned?

What change in party behavior becomes permanent?

----

6 Five Lessons

These are five lessons your character learned growing up and in training that helped shape his or her identity as a hero. Answer the prompts to discover what they are.

1. Growing up you experienced something that you never wish to revisit. It could be the desperation of extreme poverty, the isolation of social rejection, or even the guilt associated with having done something wrong.

What have you learned should be avoided at all costs? What measures do you take these days to avoid this?

2. Before you truly understood your abilities, you unintentionally caused harm with them.

What did you break or whom did you injure? How did you make up for your mistake? What did this situation teach you about managing your strength?

3. As an adolescent you stood up against something stronger than you to fight a perceived injustice.

What did you lose in pursuit of your ideals? How did this event shape your response to wrongdoing as an adult?

4. When you were a child, someone close to you hid a truth from you. As an adult you realized that person's deception.

How did the lie shape you? Did the truth hurt you? How do you approach deception as an adult?

5. During your training you risked your life for something and were rewarded for it.

How close did you come to death? What was the nature of your reward? What do you take into consideration when risking your life these days?

Ventur

Part of a character's personality is based on the company she or he prefers to keep. Imagine an app—we'll call it Ventur—designed to help adventurers find one another to form parties.

✸ **Whom does your character swipe right?**

○ **Vaelin, 349, Elf Ranger**
The two things you need to know about me are first, I love nature, and second, I hate goblins. I'm looking for a party that doesn't mind getting its hands dirty. I'm so tired of parties where the characters say they love nature but have no idea how to subsist on dewdrops. Also, if you don't want to burn a goblin camp to the ground on sight, do us both a favor and swipe left.

○ **Glorg, 32, Half-Orc Barbarian**
GLORG AM SENSITIVE SOUL. AM LOOKING 4 FELLOWSHIP MORE THAN PARTY BALANCE. NOT MIND BEING ONLY TANK AS LONG AS PEOPLE AM TANKING 4 AM GOOD FRIENDS. GLORG HEART BEEN BROKEN BEFORE BUT GLORG WILLING 2 TRY AGAIN.

○ **Truwny, 22, Gnome Bard**
What up, witches? If you want to party with me you have to dance—*no exceptions*!!! I might seem picky, but I'm actually very open-minded. I may have grown up in the country, but I live for the city. I do lutes, flutes, drums, violins, trumpets, but *never* trombones. (*Don't ask*, lol.)

○ **Jackie, 63, Human Monk**
I'm not looking for trouble. It seems like every party I'm with gets wrapped up in life-or-death battles dragging me with them. I just want to relax and see the world. I'm a huge fan of ceramic art, and I carry many vases, bowls, and plates with me everywhere. I spend a lot of time keeping up with the martial arts training I received from my monastery, but I also like to unwind. Sometimes mixing drinking and training makes everything better. Seriously though, I don't want any trouble.

O Borgar, 28, Dwarf Fighter

All you need to know: deadlift 650, bench 300, squat 425. No one under six feet.

O Seedora, 52, Half-Elf Druid

Must love wolves. Not a joke. Not an exaggeration. Swipe left if you don't love wolves. I live with a super pack of forty-six wolves, and it takes up most of my time. I want to be clear that in any party, I am alpha. Just like I am in all areas of my life. Yes, I know that the alpha model of social dynamics for wolves is dodgy science; I live with forty-six wolves. Anyway, if you love hunting, wrestling, and manually expelling anal glands for forty-six wolves, I am the druid for you.

O Hakham, 12, Tiefling Sorcerer

You didn't read that wrong. I'm twelve. Full disclosure: my village was destroyed by the dark one. I was saved at the last minute by my strange new powers. I'm adventuring to learn more about my strange past, master my powers, and avenge my lost loved ones while I come of age. My ideal party is an eclectic group of surrogate family members who insist that they work alone while welcoming me into their lives.

O Solgila, 56, Dwarf Cleric

I am a proud worshipper of the Eternal Forge. That means no beards shorter than a fist, no unshod horses, and no sunlight on Fridays. They are simple rules, but some people have trouble following them. Yes, I can heal, but you have to be righteous in the wisdom of the Forge. I consider myself a bit of a beer snob; I usually bring my own ale on quests.

○ Mardet, 34, Halfling Wizard

I've had bad luck with adventuring parties, but I'm trying again. I want a party with intellectual curiosity. I need to work with people who understand that you need to spend as much time studying ancient runes for meaning as you do searching for secret doors and treasure. I travel with a lot of books; I'm looking for a party that can help me carry them.

○ Wiris, 19, Halfling Rogue

I gotta find a party that understands *boundaries*. If something goes missing in the camp, maybe don't immediately go looking through my stuff? This should not be hard to do. Everyone wants a swift blade in the dark and a careful ear at the fire, but no one wants to trust a halfling around their packs. Message me if you are willing to trust.

○ Buwanax, 82, Human Paladin

My name is Buwanax, nice to meet you! I want to find people who are looking to make a difference in the community. If serving soup to the needy is as exciting to you as slaying dragons, then you are the person I'm looking for. I'm outgoing and love to socialize, as long as we all have time for a group prayer at the end of the night.

○ Tim, 25, Human Warlock

Yes. I made a pact with a dark god for untold power. I was young. I was dumb. I get it. There is more to me than that. I'm looking for a party that will accept me for who I am and not waste everyone's time by trying to convert me or separate me from my dark master. I want to be around people who aren't afraid of the grisly fates suffered by those who used to travel with me. I'm pretty sure that was just a very specific series of coincidences. Pure of heart only.

My Associates

Sometimes deep relationships are built around superficial details. Games tend to focus on big pictures and often lack the granularity we encounter in real-life situations. This exercise prompts you to create small details you can use to deepen character relationships. Each section challenges you to discover something new about your companions based on small things you never knew were there.

Sight

One of your companions is decorated in a style that you have never seen before. It could be clothing, makeup, or a tattoo. It is alien and alluring. You find yourself glancing at it every so often in wonder.

- Learn more about how this is made.
- Discover its cultural significance.
- Incorporate your new understanding into your own style.

Sound

One of your companions produces an unusual sound. This could be from an instrument, an accent in his voice, or a distinct pattern of his breathing. It fascinates you and gets a rise out of your animals if you own them.

- Try to reproduce or form a countermelody for the sound on an instrument you play.
- Find a name for the sound.
- Associate the sound with a feeling.

Smell

One of your companions is associated with an unusual smell. It might be a spice she puts on her food, a treatment or dye for one of her garments, a foreign perfume, or a facet of her biology.

- Discover the specific source of the scent.
- Allow the odor to lead you to develop a new skill.
- Allow the smell to change your tastes.

Across a Crowded Tavern

To someone with an eye for talent, even a character who is relatively inexperienced possesses qualities that signal potential. These prompts will help develop ways for your character to stand out from the crowd.

✸ **Choose a core character statistic and decide how it hints at your potential.**

Strength

- ○ You casually carry an object that most would move with a cart.
  - **Pick a trade:** farming, sailing, mining.
  - **Why have you brought this object to a tavern:** for delivery, for convenience on your way home, because it reminds you of a loved one?

- ○ You bear a tribute to your athletic prowess.
  - **How did you get it:** bested a famed hero, sought it on a dare, earned it while coming of age?
  - **How does it look:** forged of a dark metal, carved from strong stone, taken from a powerful beast, like a scar or tattoo?

- ○ You can cause a major calamity unintentionally through a physical power.
  - **What led you to do this:** simple clumsiness, powerful anger, misguided pride?
  - **What happens as a result:** dented metal, splintered wood, broken pottery?

Dexterity

- ○ You master a game with thoughtless ease.
  - **How did you come to play:** forced by loudmouthed friends, challenged by greedy sharks, drunken whim?
  - **This contest involves:** throwing objects, knives, darts, or axes.

- You narrowly and subtly avoided certain death.
  - **You were threatened by:** a poorly secured heavy object, a sharp object thrown through the room, a dangerous unsecured device.
  - **It looked like:** a perfectly timed fall, part of a dance, a blur as your hands moved faster than anyone could see.

- There's a trick you do idly with your fingers.
  - **It uses:** a knife, a coin, a deck of cards, an orb.
  - **It's especially impressive because:** it could cause injury, you move so many objects at once, you are doing something else at the same time—something that demands a lot of attention.

Constitution

- You have acquired a taste for a strong drink.
  - **How is your favorite drink mysterious:** it comes from far away, it frequently kills, it has cultural importance?
  - **How is it supposed to taste:** like the god's wrath, like breathing your last breath in a harsh winter storm, like the blaze of the fallen one?

- You are physically marked after surviving a seemingly impossible situation.
  - **Pick an industry you once worked in:** mining, sailing, construction.
  - **What did you suffer:** a week without food or sunlight, hours pressed under something many times your weight, pain meant to break strong people?

- You won a contest.
  - **It was a battle of:** drink, will, stamina.
  - **Your opponent:** toasted your name, cursed your name, is still recovering.

continued

Intelligence

- You enjoy a game of strategy to an extreme degree.
  - **This game involves:** cards, a board and stones, magic.
  - **You take it further by:** playing multiple opponents, playing blind, taking on a renowned challenge.

- You unraveled a seemingly impossible puzzle.
  - **The puzzle:** is a decorative box, uses ropes and rings, is inscribed on a large stone.
  - **The tavern:** uses the puzzle to dupe drunks, is named after this challenge, is run by someone who fancies himself a puzzle master.

- You spot a clever trick.
  - **It was done:** playing cards, changing money, as part of a riddle.
  - **This causes you:** mortal danger, to save a life, to run a crook out of the tavern.

Wisdom

- You are sought by a well-respected figure to offer advice.
  - **You were contacted by:** a politician, a noted religious leader, a wealthy philanthropist.
  - **It was about:** the life of a single person, the fate of many suffering people, an impossible choice.

- You prevented a devastating conflict.
  - **It was between:** a parent and child, rival families, dangerous people.
  - **You did it by:** being calm and insistent, being empathetic and firm, speaking when most would stay silent.

continued

- You avoided masked peril.
  - **You were targeted by:** a con artist, a shark, a killer.
  - **You ended up:** making some money, being the arm of justice, out of the spotlight no worse for wear.

Charisma

- You pulled off an incredible grift.
  - **It:** was a sale, got a good person out of a bad situation, won you a hefty prize.
  - **You pulled it on:** a religious official, a tax collector, the richest person in town.

- You delivered a masterful performance.
  - **It was:** musical, comedic, an impersonation.
  - **It ended with:** raucous applause, reverent silence, tears.

- You talked through bad trouble.
  - **It involved:** a sizable debt, a romantic entanglement gone wrong, a job you were supposed to do but didn't.
  - **It ended:** with other people apologizing for something you did wrong, with happy tears, with two of your enemies fighting each other.

Orphan Details

The orphan protagonist is an extremely popular trope in fantasy fiction. It makes a very convenient background for adventurers, as it cuts roots that would keep most people in one place. It also provides a simple motivation to adventure. Perhaps because it's so convenient, it is easy for an orphan character's background to be ignored. Flesh out your backstory by choosing new details from the following lists.

A Mystery

- On the day my parents were buried, the sun was blotted out by swarming crows.
- The details of my parents' deaths do not match from story to story.
- I was marked with a tattoo that has no obvious meaning.
- I heard a tale about someone whose description matches one of my parents. This person was seen long after my parents' supposed deaths.
- There is no witness account of the attack that killed my parents—just physical evidence.
- The person who left me with my caretakers only spoke a cryptic phrase.

A Person

Creating a character related to your orphan's backstory helps physicalize the story. The character can create a goal to seek, something that moves and leaves clues. Whether it is the villain who killed your parents or the mysterious figure who left your character with the people who raised you, identifying details make it easier to use that backstory in the unfolding narrative.

- He wore armor as black as night.
- In the rain and shadow, you could see her glowing eyes.
- They wore a crest with a coat of arms you have never seen.
- She had a deformity that would be instantly recognizable.
- He spoke a name that raised more questions than it answered.
- They stole an item from you that you know like your own shadow.

An Artifact

Objects provide a connection to your backstory. They can continue to pose old questions while opening new doors. Among the objects your orphan character may have are:

- A scroll written in a strange language.
- A weapon once possessed by one of your parents, now safe at your side.
- A jewel of unusual quality, which seems to sparkle even in darkness.
- The hand of the creature that killed your parents, untouched by rot.
- A heavy key with elaborate grooves.
- The journal of one of your parents, from which a few important pages are missing.

An Identity

Losing a family is inherently tragic, but it is easier to investigate if those people were well known. It gives the world reasons to embrace or impede your character's quest. Most players identify a profession for their character's deceased parents, but creating a personality for them will have a larger impact on the story. Decide if your parents were among the following:

- Revolutionary iconoclasts
- Faithful champions of their community
- Innovative thinkers at the forefront of their field
- Righteous symbols of hope and prosperity
- Cutthroat opportunists
- Outlaws and warlords

What Can You Do for Me?

You and your traveling companions have at least one goal in common. This is the major plot hook that keeps your party together. You can use that same storytelling lever to deepen and make more complex your existing relationships. This exercise will help you create character goals and enlist specific party members to aid you. Some of these activities will bring two characters closer together; others will drive them apart. Ask different party members to perform the exercise in order to create new connections.

I Want

This should be something small, perhaps frivolous. Some good examples are:

- An adjustment to my primary weapon
- To taste the meat of a beast I read about
- A song to win the heart of someone I admire
- A fine drink that I don't have to pay for

I want ______________________________.

The person most suited to help me would be ____________________

because ______________________________.

I might have to: (choose one)

- ○ Trick this person with cunning and guile
- ○ Offer him, her, or them a share of the treasure I expect to get
- ○ Apologize for an offense I caused
- ○ Teach the secret of my trade

continued

I Need

This should be related to a personal goal your character consciously pursues. Something related to your backstory or main character arc is perfect for this. It should be narrow in scope, a goal that could realistically be accomplished in a few sessions. Some good examples are:

- To identify the mysterious jewel given to me by my mentor
- To find stories of the killer I plan to bring to justice
- To research a better component for a complicated spell
- To create a convincing forgery for a noble title

I need ____.

The person most suited to help me would be ____________________

because ____.

I might have to: (choose one)

- ○ Convince him this is a righteous cause
- ○ Pay her with a favor in kind
- ○ Do something to earn their respect
- ○ Reveal a secret about myself to her

I Long For

This should be a desire your character is not consciously aware of. It is a long-term character transformation that might play out over a significant period. It may be a goal that is completely unattainable but is interesting to chase after. Some good examples are:

- The parent I never had
- Peace with the person I used to be
- A person to share my life with
- A reason to keep fighting

I long for ______________________________.

The person most suited to help me would be ______________________

because ______________________________.

I may have to: (choose one)

- ○ Expose that which I wish to conceal the most
- ○ Swear to this person an oath I would die to keep
- ○ Betray a part of my personal moral code
- ○ Steal something that can never be returned

A Matter of Status

One of the most important dynamics in relationships between characters is status. Status dictates how different characters view and treat one another. It can be based on concrete factors such as social standing, material wealth, physical power, and age, or it can be determined by subtle factors like character motivation, personal history, or physical attraction. This section will help you unpack some of the methods you can use to play with status.

Discovery

Imagine everyone in your character's party has a number between one and ten floating over their heads. This number represents their status. Here are some examples of what might give someone a high status or a low status. Read through them and assign what you believe the status to be for your party's social dynamic.

High Status

- This person is trustworthy.
- This person is strong.
- This person is wise.
- You would not want to risk upsetting this person.
- There is an advantage in keeping this person happy.
- This person possesses valuable skills.
- This person is attractive.
- This person is charming.
- This person has shown courage.
- This is someone you want to impress.
- Her opinion matters.
- He holds power in society.

Low Status

- This person is weak.
- Her opinion is uninformed.
- They cannot be trusted.
- When push comes to shove, she will back down.

continued

- This person is easy to fool.
- There is much this person cannot see.
- This person is a deviant.
- This person is likely to embarrass himself and others.
- Upsetting this person carries no real consequences.
- This person is ugly.
- This person does not express herself well.
- This person is a coward.

Based on those statements, try picking a number for each character in your party. This does not tell you if a character is good or bad, but it does give a clue as to how other characters treat her, him, or them.

Agreement

One of the most difficult things for new players to negotiate is which character in a given scene has high status. In a game all the players are protagonists, and for the most part, we are conditioned to expect protagonists to overcome obstacles. That means it's pretty common for PCs to approach every situation as though they have high status, even when it makes storytelling more difficult. When everyone in a scene agrees who has high and low status, it can make it easier to choose how to play out that scene.

Imagine an adventuring party is making a purchase from a merchant. The scene has different possibilities based on who has high status.

High-Status Party/Low-Status Merchant

- The party can make extra demands for its purchase.
- The merchant will attempt to keep the party in the shop.
- The merchant may offer unprompted gifts or compliments.
- The party reasons with logic in the interest of "fairness."
- Every flaw in the merchandise provokes an emotional response from the merchant.

continued

High-Status Merchant/Low-Status Party

- The merchant can request additional and unusual forms of payment if the party has insufficient gold.
- The merchant may be dismissive, impatient, or openly hostile as the party continues to shop.
- The party uses emotional appeals and asks for exceptions in the interest of "kindness."
- Every flaw in the merchandise is ignored or dismissed by the merchant.

A transactional scene can affect the story in one of two ways: either the party will make a purchase, or it won't. Attempting a high-status move in a scene where your party does not have high status can be fun, but it won't move the scene forward. For example, asking a merchant to add more to a purchase he already insists you cannot afford won't get you closer to completing the transaction. Playing into low status by bursting into tears might. Recognizing what status you bring to the table in any situation will help you avoid roadblocks in storytelling.

Transformation

Status is not set in stone and can evolve as a story progresses and characters grow. The captain of the watch who originally dismissed your party members as rabble-rousers may grow to respect them after they save the town from danger. A troublesome vizier might become accommodating and demure if he worries you have compromising evidence against them. Your party might treat the fighter differently once it discovers she is the princess in disguise.

Transformation can play out slowly as major elements of the story unfold and your party grows in strength. It can also shift quickly within a scene when new information is revealed. To change status, you have to introduce information that changes the scene. Referring back to our example of the merchant, let's look at actions that would or wouldn't change a party from low to high status.

continued

Actions That Would Not Change Status

- Threats that the merchant believes could not reasonably be carried out
- Attempts to appeal to qualities the merchant has not displayed
- Offers of goods the merchant has no need for
- Promises of fame or renown that mean nothing to the merchant

Actions That Could Change Status

- Realistic intimidation based on actions the merchant knows you are capable of
- Directed emotional appeals based on information you have about the merchant's personality
- Offer of a specific item the merchant wants
- Revealing of titles or accomplishments that the merchant respects

Being aware of your status lets you control the momentum of social scenes by knowing how to move forward.

What Drives You Forward?

Here's an exercise to help develop the ways in which your core motivations spur your decisions. Answer the prompts to create deep motivations for your character.

Fighting for Your Life

You are at death's door. Your breath is shallow and ragged. Your joints cry and ache. Every physical part of you longs to lie down and rest, come what may.

What image appears in your mind that inspires you to keep fighting?

Without a Clue

The trail is cold. Following every clue has led you back to the same place of uncertainty from which you started. You can feel icy dread creeping over you as you consider the possibility of reexamining everything that brought you to this point.

What physical object do you instinctively reach for in this moment? What comfort does it bring?

Lost Your Way

In the pursuit of righting wrongs, the line between good and evil has become blurred. You have done things you could never have imagined doing before, but you are not sure if that crossed a line.

What words guide you toward your moral center? Who said them?

Facing the Unknown

You are faced with a locked chest deep within a dungeon. On your journey down, you have faced many clever traps and seen valuable rewards.

What treasure that could be hidden inside makes you want to open the chest?

Social Unrest

You and your party are facing a serious problem and cannot agree on a solution. You have argued until you are blue in the face, and the temptation to go your own way is strong.

What moment from your past makes you try again to reach the other members?

Where I'm From

Create a snapshot of where you came from and how it shaped the person you became. Pick details to inspire you and use them to answer the prompts.

✸ Choose a Size for Your Town

O Metropolis

A sprawling city with thousands, perhaps millions of inhabitants. People and goods from many different places around the globe make their way through a place like this. Despite being surrounded by people, it is easy to feel alone and lost here. Wealth and poverty live beside each other in stark juxtaposition. Infrastructure is vast and almost impossible for a single person to comprehend.

O Town

Home to hundreds or perhaps even a thousand inhabitants. Although there is a sharp social division between the ruling and serving classes, no one is separated by more than two or three degrees. Even the people not known to you by name are familiar in appearance. There are many organized institutions that make life in this place possible.

O Village

Home to at most a few hundred. It is easily possible to know everyone by name and profession. There can be no real anonymity because anyone trying to conceal her or his business quickly becomes known for being mysterious. Settlement is permanent, if disorganized. Many structures are grouped together out of convenience rather than careful planning.

O Tribe

Home to at most a few dozen. Civic and familial bonds are blurred. Community obligations are approached with grave seriousness. A tribe can be tied to a permanent location or an idea carried by nomadic people.

○ Pack

A small group. Even if not related by blood, members treat one another as family, with all the emotion, obligation, and loyalty that come with it. A pack can weave in and out of larger communities or shun civilization altogether.

Where Did You Call Home?

For some characters this is a permanent room or residence. For others it is an abstract feeling about certain periods of safety and stability. Finding those truths for your character will help you understand how he or she approaches the concept of home on the road.

Where did you most often sleep? ____________________

What did you need to do to maintain it? ____________________

Did it protect you and what you cared for? ____________________

Do you long for it now? ____________________

Where Did People Socialize?

There are places of merriment and relaxation everywhere. This exercise will examine one of particular importance to your character.

Choose two:

- ○ The hearth was always warm when the wind was cold.
- ○ The music moves your heart even in memory.
- ○ The owner was wise or at least gave advice as though he were.
- ○ The food was cooked with quiet pride.
- ○ It always seemed to hold a dazzling glow.
- ○ Being there faded the weight of obligation just enough.
- ○ You watched more than you took part.

But... (choose one)

- You rarely left with a full belly.
- Everything was watered down.
- It drew the most dangerous thugs and criminals.
- You were often present but never welcome.
- The spell it cast wore off all too quickly.
- You risked everything to be there.
- You could never ignore where the money went.

What was it officially titled? ____________________

What did people call it? ____________________

What Did People Respect?

Where people assign their respect shows us what they value. To get an idea of the values held by the people of your hometown, select everything you believe is true.

People respected...

- Power
- Authority
- Cunning
- Nature
- Wealth
- Ambition
- The divine
- One another
- The law
- Life
- Love
- Strength
- Wisdom
- Knowledge
- Skill
- Discovery
- Justice

Are these values you hold today? ____________________

How do your personal values differ?

____

____

____

Who Was in Charge?

Any collective is under the rule of some other force. Even those who reject rule by other creatures are subject to the will of law or nature. This exercise explores the relationship between your character and authority.

The force in charge of your hometown: (choose two)

- O Was a thing of power and majesty
- O Never spoke but was always heard
- O Ruled with wisdom
- O Demanded loyalty
- O Understood kindness
- O Worked diligently
- O Was controlled by another
- O Earned your hatred
- O Was the product of divine right

But... (choose one)

- O It was worthy of respect.
- O It killed without thought.
- O It made many mistakes.
- O It aged and died.
- O It was eventually overthrown.
- O It expected much from me.

What was the ruler's name?

Based on this experience, when you picture a ruler, what does he, she, or they look like?

If given the chance to lead, whom would you emulate?

What Was Your Place?

Perhaps the single thing that most dramatically colors your character's perception of place of origin is her or his place in it. It is useless to know your character was a student, noble, or blacksmith if you do not understand how he or she feels about it. Finding this will solidify what your character is running away from and toward.

I was: (choose one)

- O Safe
- O Respected
- O Worshipped
- O Ignored
- O Hated
- O Feared
- O Mistreated

My duty was to: (choose one)

- O Learn
- O Grow
- O Protect
- O Provide
- O Serve
- O Die

Which I: (choose one)

- O Humbly accepted
- O Regretfully fulfilled
- O Actively resisted
- O Desperately ran from
- O Painfully failed
- O Continue to carry out

If you could return to this role, would you?

- O Not if the chains of hell dragged me back.
- O No, I am now unworthy.
- O No, I am too important.
- O I don't know.
- O Yes, with great sorrow.
- O Yes, but this time would be different.
- O Yes, with great pride.

Finders Keepers

This exercise puts you in a tense situation where time is critical. What are you willing to risk to discover the truth and aid a stranger? A hero might stop to try and help someone in need, exposing themselves to danger. A less remarkable traveler might keep to themselves and stay safe. An unscrupulous wretch might take a risk only for personal gain. Every action has consequences, and the more time you spend, the greater the danger. Choose your actions carefully and answer the prompts to see how your choices affect you. **You find a body in the road. It is beginning to grow dark, and this region is dangerous at night.**

Identify

✸ **Try to discover who this stranger might be.**

- After looking at this person, you believe there are three people in a nearby town who might fit his description.
  - A small-time highwayman is said to stalk these woods, ambushing merchants on the way to town.
    - ○ Search for proof. (*15 minutes...*) The highwayman was shot with more than one arrow over the years and should have scars on his chest.

    Rolling 5–6 on a d6 confirms this hunch.
  - An old watchman left a few days ago to hunt a highwayman in the woods.
    - ○ Search for proof. (*2 minutes...*) The watchman was married and wore a brass ring on his wrist as was the region's custom.

    Rolling 3–4 on a d6 confirms this hunch.
  - A ranger who occasionally sells furs in town is said to hunt not far from here.
    - ○ Search for proof. (*5 minutes...*) The ranger saved a family from an attacking wolf a few years back and has a scar on his leg.

    Rolling 1–2 on a d6 confirms this hunch.

Investigate

 **What do you wish to examine?**

POSSESSIONS

You find a pouch, a neat roll of parchment stained with blood, and a copper shield in the man's chest pocket, as well as a holy symbol.

- Read the parchment. (*15 minutes...*) "To the stranger who may find me: I have failed in my quest. I cannot claim that I was a noble soul, but I seek judgment only from my god. Please take a coin from my pouch to place (*blood has blurred some words*) under my tongue, two coins to return to my (*blood obscures more*) and the rest as payment for your trouble. —Cassidy."
- Look in the pouch. (*2 minutes...*) You find coins: one gold, two silver, ten copper pieces.
- Investigate the holy symbol. (*20 minutes...*) This symbol belongs to a thieves' church. They worship a god of fortune. It is said their god "hates fire, loves any who speaks with gold, judges a tongue of silver, and ignores the sound of copper."
    - Consult the *Adventurer's Almanac*. (*30 minutes...*) It is not uncommon for a watchman to carry a symbol of the god of thieves, as "a thief knows where to find his own." Many officers are buried with an old-style badge under their tongues to shield them from the thief lord's wrath.
- Investigate. (*10 minutes...*) The copper shield is a discontinued symbol denoting rank in the watch. It was discontinued because the simple design was too easy to counterfeit.

THE BODY

You see a wound on this poor soul's chest and what looks like a tattoo running up his arm. His hand is missing four fingers.

- O The wound. *(20 minutes...)* This is most likely the result of the blow that killed this traveler. It could have been made with an unusual weapon or strange beastly appendage. It is beyond your ability to know which. Whatever did this was tremendously strong. Most likely this stranger died quickly.
- O The tattoo. *(10 minutes...)* This is an elaborate strip winding symbols and lines. There appears to be a pattern to it, but it would take some time to work out the meaning.
  - O *(30 minutes...)* After deciphering runes and letters from various languages, you find that this tattoo denotes affiliation with the thieves' guild. Based on what you were able to put together, this person must have been a high-ranking member.
- O The hand. *(10 minutes...)* Four fingers were lost from this person's left hand a few years ago. Although they have grown pale, the scars make you wince. The implement responsible for this must have been sharp and regular since the cut is clean.
  - O Consult the *Adventurer's Almanac*. *(30 minutes...)* The thieves' guild punishes ex-members by removing fingers from their left hands. This is to prevent ex-thieves from using their skills outside the guild. It also signals to other thieves the former member's status. A person missing a single finger may simply be someone who retired early. A person missing four likely betrayed the guild to the law.

TEND TO THE BODY

- O *(20 minutes...)* Burn it to keep it from being ravaged by beasts.
- O *(1 hour...)* Cover it in rocks to mark its place.
- O *(1.5 hours...)* Dig a grave and perform a rite that your beliefs tell you brings the dead good fortune.
- O *(0 minutes...)* Leave it to rot.

Add all the time you spent investigating this body.

Roll two d10s to simulate a d100, sometimes referred to as a d%. Choose one die to represent the ones column, and the other to represent tens; this roll will give you a result from 1–100. Add ten to the roll for each hour spent exposed on the road. If your roll goes above fifty, you are attacked by the thing that killed the traveler. Fight or flee.

What, if anything, do you do with the possessions found on the body?

Do you tell anyone about what you found? If so, whom?

Well Worn

The objects carried by heroes are tools and a form of self-expression. Define your look by adding a wealth of small details to your equipment through rolling and answering these prompts.

Handed Down

This object came to you from someone you look up to. Yours are not the first or second hands to touch it.

This is: (choose or roll a d6)

1. A tool used in a trade I learned
2. A weapon I have mastered
3. An instrument I am skilled with
4. A book bound with skill
5. A pack, sturdy and strong
6. A piece of precious jewelry

How has it changed since it came into your possession?

Who do you think of when you hold it?

Made Mine

This was bought from a shop or merchant. There are many people with items such as this, but you have altered it to make it unique.

How did this item change? (roll a d6)

1. I altered it to fit my size.
2. I broke it down for parts to make something new.
3. I decorated it to fit my tastes.
4. I broke it accidentally but found a new use for the result.
5. I made it deadly.
6. I gave it a secret.

When people discover the origin of this item, is the change a source of pride or embarrassment?

Do you ever plan to replace it? --

Made New

This is something you created yourself. It took time and care to create whether or not it was created with much skill.

Why did you make this? (roll a d6)

1. Out of need
2. For self-expression
3. Out of boredom
4. To honor a memory
5. To prove myself
6. To keep in practice

Where do you keep this object? --

What plans do you have for it?

Five Things You Packed but Shouldn't Have

Examine your character's inexperience by examining items that really don't belong in an adventurer's pack.

1. Growing up, you were taught that a specific item was important to your identity. On the road you have found little use for it. Every time you see it among your belongings, you make an excuse to keep it, though each time, those excuses are harder to find.

What is this, and where did you get it?

---

2. This was part of an old superstition you were taught as a child. It has since proven to be untrue.

What is it, and when did you try to use it?

---

3. When first venturing out, you grabbed this. It seemed like something useful you would need on the road. You are still waiting for the perfect opportunity to pull it out.

What is it, and when do you plan to use it?

---

4. You purchased this intending to learn how to use it. You keep putting off that learning experience. Now throwing it away would be admitting you will never gain that skill.

What is it, and how long would it actually take you to learn how to use it?

---

5. This is an article of clothing for which you have a sentimental fondness. It is damaged to the point of being unusable, or it could be replaced by a more suitable item.

What is it, and who made it?

Of the Cloth

Use these charts to help players visualize different ways to play a character whose religion is a major theme.

Mission

One of the major ways religion gets expressed in a game is how you choose to answer a divine calling. Your alignment only tells you what effect you want to have on the world. This chart will tell you how to approach those goals.

Choose how you answer a divine calling:

● **Evangelical**	You hope to grow your religious order and convert the faithless. You feel you are on the right path when you welcome new people to the flock.
● **Enlightening**	You want the wisdom of your faith and your god's message to be present in the world, but you don't need dedication from the people you deliver your message to. It is fine to have someone be faithless or worship another god so long as your message is one of comfort.
● **Healing**	Your work is primarily to right wrongs and soothe suffering. For right to triumph, the world must be able to erase the effects of wrong.
● **Crusading**	You proactively seek to conquer what you see as the ills of the world. You upset status quos and try to make changes according to your values.

continued

Relationship

Religious characters do not all feel the same way about their religions, and not all deities treat their champions in the same way. Even within the same faith, two characters can have a radically different experience of what that faith means.

Choose how you practice your faith:

○ **Devoted**	On this end of the spectrum, you are unshakably committed to your beliefs—the sort of person who dies suffering and gets named a saint.
○ **Questioning**	You are skeptical of aspects of your faith or church. You are the sort of person who inspires a reformation or weeds out corruption.
○ **Favor**	Your deity is a comforting presence that admires your work. You find fortune in hardship and receive help when you need it.
○ **Trial**	Your deity constantly tests your faith and asks for sacrifice. It wishes to see you emerge victorious but never makes it easy.

19 Five Fears

The true measure of courage is not to face danger fearlessly but to face fear and overcome it. Heroes without fear lack an important emotional tool to add weight to their stories. This exercise will help you discover that fear makes you stronger and more interesting.

The Body

One of the most obvious fears to confront an adventurer with is that of physical harm. After all, a huge portion of the job is risking danger. Pain and death are obvious and appropriate fears that most adventurers will face often. It may add flavor to some characters to make this a fear of specific injury: for instance, a bard may be terrified of an injured hand, which will affect her music. Some characters may need an even subtler approach. A strong fighter may fear their body aging, thus losing their defining trait. A character obsessed with strength can even fear an inadequacy that does not exist, frightened of a weakness she does not possess.

✸ **Carefully consider what your character feels is important and what he or she would do to protect that. For instance:**

- O Pain
- O Weakness
- O Inadequacy
- O Injury
- O Sickness
- O Death

The Mind

The most powerful tool any adventurer has in her arsenal is her mind, since it controls how she puts her skills to use. It can also work against her, constructing invisible enemies and threats out of harmless things. Shadows can be signs of lurking horror; coincidence can be a sign of a superior enemy; an oddly phrased sentence can be a sign of conspiracy. Adventurers make calculations about danger out of necessity. Fear lies in how they draw those conclusions and react to them. The mind is also the space where characters catalog their plans and resources. Any anxiety about failure, readiness, or progress is felt through the mind. Certain heroes are dependent on their minds in ways others are not. For a wizard, his mind and ability to study are paths to power. It is easy to tie this story to fears of inadequacy and anxiety over sense of self. Fears of the mind are less visceral than others, but they carry no less weight.

To create a mind-based fear for your character, consider what you know and focus on the dangers you find most important. For instance:

- Anxiety
- Lack of preparation
- Feeling lost
- Post-traumatic stress
- Lack of valuable information
- Existential dread

The Soul

The world of fantasy offers boundless possibilities for exploring spiritual themes. A lot of what is abstract in real life takes concrete form in fantasy. It is very possible to play a character who simply fears evil as a force. A story about good and evil on a conceptual level becomes more grounded when you have a character embody those concepts. Evil is very easy to understand when it can swing a sword at you. You can even create internal conflict by exploring the thought process of a good person for whom violence is an unavoidable aspect of life. Fearing personal corruption is a great way to add weight to actions and decisions your character must make.

To construct a spiritual fear, ask difficult questions about your character's beliefs and behavior. Create an emotional attachment to his or her sense of justice and find the areas where there are no easy answers. For instance:

- The nature of evil
- The fragility of virtue
- A specific evil person
- Personal corruption
- Crisis of faith
- Cosmic horror à la H.P. Lovecraft

The Heart

Emotional storytelling is the core of character-driven fiction. The way you interact with other characters drives a great deal of the story. Rejection is an easy theme around which to build fear. Our world is already fraught with social strife surrounding appearance and acceptance. Adding features like tusks, tails, and otherworldly fire to other characters or NPCs (non-player characters) makes differences more overt and easier to play with. Facing rejection is especially terrifying when one's way of life depends on trusting other people. On the other side of the coin, intimacy is another common heroic fear. Allowing yourself to care about others makes the pain of loss more pronounced and opens you up to new vulnerabilities. Fear of intimacy raises the stakes on otherwise mundane interactions.

To construct a fear of the heart, focus on a social interaction and what would happen if something went wrong. For instance:

- Rejection
- Intimacy
- Loneliness
- Personal awkwardness
- Loss
- Social pressures to succeed

The Beast

Despite being abstract, the beast is probably the most commonly represented fear in storytelling. It is based around the unknown and unknowable causing harm. The most obvious manifestation of the beast is monsters: the awful things that lurk in dungeons with sharp teeth and steely claws. It is easy to play a character who fears a specific type of monster. Almost every creature found in a monster manual, or bestiary, is individually terrifying, and it is easy to empathize with a character who sees monsters that way. The beast is also a central aspect of cosmic horror, where forbidden truths unravel stable aspects of reality to make our world unstable and unsafe. There is also an element of the beast in the fears that drive hatred and bigotry. Those who are ignorant and fear what they do not understand are in thrall to the beast.

To construct a fear of the beast, think of what your character does not know and find a way to make that dangerous. Focus on the alien and outwardly horrific to find the shape of the beast. For instance:

- Monstrous appearance
- Dangerous abilities
- Forbidden knowledge
- Alien cultures and practices
- Unfamiliar devices
- Uncontained power

What Does It Mean to Be...?

Some games call for you to select a race or species. On the surface, these provide physical characteristics and options to personalize your character. You can also use a character's race to create a cultural identity and define aspects of your setting. This exercise will help you construct an identity around your character's race, which you can play into or against.

I am a ....

Make choices to flesh out your relationship with your species.

OUR POPULATION IS: (CHOOSE ONE)

- O Overpopulated
- O Thriving
- O Unremarkable
- O Underrepresented
- O Dying out

COMPARED TO OTHER COMMON RACES, OUR STATURE IS: (CHOOSE ONE)

- O Larger
- O Average
- O Smaller

GENERALLY, STRANGERS LOOK AT ME AND FEEL: (CHOOSE ALL THAT APPLY)

- O Fear
- O Awe
- O Amusement
- O Infatuation
- O Anger
- O Pity
- O Disgust
- O Safe

continued

MOST PLACES I TRAVEL: (CHOOSE ONE)

- O I am worshipped
- O I am ostracized
- O I am not noticed
- O I am a considered a threat

Write a statement about your identity based on the prompt.

My parents taught me

My church taught me

Society taught me

Which of these lessons is most important to your identity?

WHEN DEALING WITH MY RACE, I USUALLY: (CHOOSE ONE)

- O Don't think about it
- O Try to ignore it
- O Agonize over it
- O Place emphasis on it

Private Mysteries

Game worlds can be truly impressive acts of creation. There are truths that even the people who created them and the characters who live in them don't know. This exercise encourages you to ask and answer questions about the setting of your game world. As a player you can make it your character's mission to discover truths; as a game master (GM) you can muse on specific setting elements.

Mundane

Things that are a part of your character's everyday life sometimes defy explanation. Basic history and infrastructure in a fantasy world can be a captivating line of inquiry.

Who supplies mundane equipment for the wizard's college?

Are there uniform robes for students? ----------------

- Who manufactures them? ----------------
- Who cleans them? ----------------
- How much does the school spend dressing its students? ----------

What sort of writing implement do students favor? ----------

- Is it a quill? If so, from what creature? If it is not a quill, why favor something else?

- How often do writing instruments need to be replaced? ____________
- How many does the average student use in a year? ____________
- How does the supplier source its materials? ____________

How does the school feed its students? ____________

- Who is the head chef? ____________
- Who is in charge of ordering supplies? ____________
- Who does the school purchase its food from? ____________
- Is the school getting a good deal? ____________

How does the largest city in the setting deal with waste?

____

Does it have a sewage system? ____________

- Is flooding a problem? ____________
- Who designed the city's infrastructure? ____________

Is there an organization in charge of refuse management? ____________

- How does this organization collect trash? ____________
- What does it do with it? ____________
- What would happen if the workers were to go on strike? ____________

Who makes the world's greatest wines?

Where do they grow their crops? ______

- Are the fruits remarkable? ______
- Is the soil special? ______
- What is the weather like? ______

Do their storage techniques vary? ______

- Do they use magic? ______
- Where do they age the wine? ______
- Has anything ever been stolen? ______

Who insists on their superiority? ______

- Could their loyalty be politically motivated? ______
- When did this wine become popular? ______
- How large is the wine trade in the region where it is produced?

  ______

Germane

Looking into certain world information can provide you with story options down the road.

Who could make the finest version of your favored weapon?

Is there a technique of forging that makes one blade superior to another?

- How long has it been in use? ----------
- Who developed it? ----------
- What do blacksmiths brag about when they describe their work?

Is there a school or army renowned for fighting in your style? ----------

- Where does it get its weapons? ----------
- What does the master of arms use? ----------
- Are your needs different from those of the average fighter?

How long does it take to create a weapon of good quality? ----------

- Is there a ceremony that accompanies weapon forging?

What is the most remote settlement in the world?

Who lives there?

- How many people call it home?
- How do they maintain their population?
- Do they depend on the outside world at all?

How old is it?

- Who founded it?
- Why did they stay?
- Who is the best historian for this subject?

Is it dangerous?

- Are the threats climate based, creature based, or both?
- Is there special infrastructure that makes life there possible?
- Is something that poses a threat also something that promotes life?

Who controls the most powerful army in the world?

Is this a matter of debate? ---

Where do they recruit soldiers? ---

- How do they train their officers? ---
- When do soldiers retire? ---
- Do they employ mercenaries? ---

Who supplies them with food and weapons? ---

- How do they transport supplies? ---
- Which relationships do they depend on to make this possible?

- Is any of their equipment unique? ---

What was their most recent loss? ---

- What do you think caused it? ---
- Did this greatly impact their approach to warfare? ---
- How did their enemy capitalize on this defeat? ---

Who is the wealthiest person in the setting?

How did he or she acquire his or her wealth?

- How long did it take to amass?
- Was it all legal?
- How is it primarily held?

What is his or her most recent endeavor?

- Why did he or she devote time to this?
- Is it providing a clear benefit?
- What do most people think of it?

Does he, she, or they have rivals?

- Are there people who could cut off access to controlled resources?
- Who presents a physical threat to his, her, or their holdings?
- Who is the second wealthiest individual in the world?

Prophecy Half-Remembered

In a fantasy setting, prophecies can birth nations, unseat tyrants, and shape the world. Of course, in a place where magic is common and mystics hold power, you'll find them everywhere from all sorts of qualified and unqualified sources.

 **Use a d6 to roll random elements of a prophecy you know and think about from time to time.**

I HEARD FROM...

1. A person at a crossroads
2. An old sage
3. A dream
4. The bones (or another fortune-telling system)
5. A drunk
6. An oracle

	When...	If...	"I heard..."
1	The age of men has passed	The moon shines red	A horse that walks backward
2	In the fourth hour of the third day of the second month of the first year	The snow covers all the earth	A white crow
3	All hope is lost	The sun fails to rise	Thirty starlings
4	You hear the voice of the wind	A fox speaks with the voice of a man	Losing your shadow
5	A star shines brighter than the moon	A child is born before kings	A dog with no teeth
6	You draw your last breath	Color fills the sky	Eyes the color of emeralds

continued

MEANS/SIGNALS

Tragedy	Fortune
1 A beloved leader will die	1 The death of a tyrant
2 Crops will fail	2 A time of plenty
3 Waters will rise	3 The birth of a champion
4 The dead will rise	4 You will have extraordinary luck
5 Poverty and ruin will stalk the land	5 You are sure to find love
6 The apocalypse will occur	6 A wish will be granted

IT CAN BE PREVENTED BY…/IT WILL BE CAUSED BY…

1 Someone of a description matching one of your companions
2 Someone of a description matching yourself
3 An unpopular group
4 The chosen one
5 One who holds stars in her hands
6 A coalition of warring nations

On the Line

Adventurers put their lives on the line every day, but that behavior had to start somewhere. This exercise will help you outline how you learned to do this.

 **Choose or use a d6 to randomly roll elements of the first time you risked your life for something and describe what you created once the scene was clear.**

IT HAPPENED...

1. When I was only a child
2. When I was still learning to read
3. Before I could call myself an adult
4. When I first left home
5. Before I mastered my craft
6. Only very recently

I DID IT TO...

1. Get something valuable
2. Impress someone
3. Prove I was not a coward
4. Test my abilities
5. Save someone important
6. Get out of a worse situation

IT COULD HAVE BEEN WORSE...

1. I broke a few bones
2. I got a nasty scar
3. I lost something small
4. I lost a limb
5. I occasionally have flashbacks
6. I got away unscathed

I LOOK BACK AND THINK…

1. About what a fool I was
2. How lucky I am
3. If only I had been stronger then
4. I did everything I could
5. I wouldn't have it any other way
6. I should have tried it sooner

Think of the closest call during this situation and describe the scene.

Red Flags

You are desperate for work and in need of money, but not every job is one you want to take. Each item that follows adds a new fact about a job your character is offered.

Decide when you think the work is too much trouble.

- You are approached by a stranger.
- He wears a hood to hide his face.
- He speaks in cool, oily sentences, which drip with easy charisma.
- He speaks in a rasping voice.
- He has a tattoo with unfamiliar symbols just barely visible at the edge of his sleeve.
- He warns you it could be a dangerous job.
- The work he describes seems almost too simple.
- Your skills and experience are uniquely suited to the task.
- You know of only one other sellsword who took work like this.
- The reward is three times what you expect for this sort of work.
- The job involves travel away from civilization for a few days.
- More than one adventuring party has gone missing in this region.
- You have heard rumors of a death cult called the Crimson Dawn operating in the woods not far from here.
- The robe the stranger wears is a shade of red.
- The bartender has been glancing nervously toward your table throughout the night.
- The sellsword you know who took a job like this has been bragging about her good fortune for weeks.
- The stranger tends to chuckle to himself while he speaks.
- The chuckle turns into a full laugh.
- Occasionally, the laugh slips into a maniacal shriek.
- It could be the light, but you thought you saw the stranger's eyes glow red.
- Inside the bottom of the wooden mug you just emptied, the word *run* has been scratched.
- At the first sign of your confidence fading, the stranger offers to double his payment.

continued

- Laughing nervously, the sellsword you met approaches the table and loudly declares, "I'm so jealous of how rich you are about to be. I wish I was a wise and talented negotiator like you."
- The stranger adds, "We're looking forward to paying you your reward."
- The sellsword elbows him in the side.
- Two watchmen enter the bar and peer around the room. Without warning, the stranger and the sellsword drop beneath the table.
- The watchmen leave, and the stranger and the sellsword get up.
- They look at you guiltily.
- "Sorry about that. We were just—" the sellsword starts before being interrupted by the stranger, who says hastily, "We were kissing."
- The sellsword shoots a pointed look at the stranger, who continues, "With our human mouths."
- You hear a heavy boot stomp under the table as the stranger yelps. The sellsword laughs and growls, "You know humans, always kissing with their mouths."
- "We lack the sexual enlightenment to reproduce through a spawning pool, so we kiss under tables," the stranger adds helpfully.
- The sellsword rubs her temples.
- The stranger winks.
- The stranger's eyes are *definitely* glowing.
- The watchmen reenter the tavern, and one of them announces to the room, "Hey, everyone, we're looking for two members of the Crimson Dawn death cult rumored to be in the area. They dupe foolish adventurers into entering the forest, using promises of wealth. Their victims suffer horrible fates. Worse than death. If you think you have seen one of them, let us know." The watchmen exit, seemingly in a hurry.
- The stranger and the sellsword once again emerge from under the table.
- "Kissing sure is a pleasant way to use a human mouth," the stranger says. He extends his hand to a bard sitting at an adjacent table for a high five before the sellsword violently pulls him back to the table.

Damn Merlinials

As often happens, older generations of adventurers look down on and resent those just starting out. Choose details about your setting and use them to answer the prompts to define the divide between old and young adventurers.

Before we get started, establish the truth of this world:

- There are more/fewer adventurers now than before.
- A wise/cruel/controversial leader sits on the throne.
- It is a time of relative peace/upheaval/brutal conflict.

Technology

A new piece of technology fundamentally changed the way your world works before you entered the adventuring profession. It could be related to heroism or have nothing to do with it.

To determine what it is, choose two:

- It is magical in nature.
- It created a new industry.
- It made people safer.
- It exposed the world to new dangers.
- It is something people use every day.
- It caused widespread controversy.

What is it called?

In a sentence, what does it do?

How do older generations opt out of the changes it brings?

Social

A new social trend is common mostly among younger generations.

Choose two:

- It changes the way people approach sex.
- It involves controlled substances.
- It is related to music or dance.
- It is currently illegal.
- It has been relentlessly commercialized.
- It is made possible by magic.
- It has been condemned by most churches.

No matter what choices you made, you also understand it to be mostly harmless.

What is it called?

Did you enjoy it the first time you tried it?

Fashion

Fashion is always evolving. Even without seeing someone's face, it is easy to tell how old an adventurer is by looking at his, her, or their gear.

To determine the current trend, pick one:

- Pragmatic and simple
- Flashy and detailed
- Sleek and cold
- Elegant and warm

Choose an accessory:

- Belts
- Capes
- Scabbards
- Bracers
- Scarves
- Gloves
- Boots
- Hats

Think about the world's economy and choose one:

- It is a way for the poor to express themselves.
- It costs two months' savings.
- The debt required to attain it is a drop in the bucket compared to what you already owe.

Create a word for the style based on the descriptor you find most appropriate:

- **Counterculture:** Choose a harsh-sounding single-syllable word. If it doesn't seem right, add *-punk* as a suffix.
- **Bohemian:** Create a delicate nonsense word and add *art* before it.
- **Stark:** Choose a violent word and add the suffix *-ist* or *-house*.
- **Debutant:** Create a word or phrase that is at least three syllables and add the suffix *-coco* or *-ic*.

Language

It is easy to tell who is old and who is young based on the way people speak.

✸ **The younger generation:**

- O Complicates language
- O Simplifies language

✸ **There is a new influence on speech that comes from increased interaction with: (choose one)**

- O Elves
- O Dwarfs
- O Orcs
- O Humans
- O Creatures beyond our plane
- O Creatures no taller than three feet
- O A being who is powerful and charismatic

✎ **You use this word as an expletive when things are dangerous:**

✎ **You use this word to call someone attractive:**

✎ **You call older heroes who are about to retire:**

Rival

On your journey you will face many foes. Some will cause pain; others will make you groan in irritation. Only one spurs you forward at every pass, delicately walking the line between friend and foe. This exercise will help craft an outline for a rival your GM can bring to life.

 **Roll a d6 or choose the details you think suit you best.**

WE MET... (CHOOSE ONE)

1. When I was a child
2. In training
3. On the road
4. In a dungeon
5. In a tavern
6. Running from the same threat

WE CANNOT STAND EACH OTHER DESPITE... (CHOOSE ONE)

1. Practicing the same craft
2. Being bound by blood
3. Once being great friends
4. Having the same master
5. Having similar taste
6. Saving each other's lives

✸ **We first fought... (choose one)**

- O After I corrected him, her, or them
- O Over the same prize
- O For the attention of the same person
- O In a situation that nearly got us killed
- O Because of pride
- O Over something unbelievably petty, but I secretly... (choose one)
  - O Admire his, her, or their strength
  - O Envy his or her privilege
  - O Want his or her approval
  - O Crave his, her, or their attention
  - O Trust him or her with my life
  - O Find him or her attractive

continued

MY RIVAL...

Looks	Behaves
1 Stylish	1 Impulsively
2 Oafish	2 Thoughtfully
3 Dangerous	3 Cruelly
4 Wealthy	4 Haughtily
5 Frail	5 Nobly
6 Like me	6 Like me
Dresses	**Fights**
1 With style	1 With a demon's strength
2 In unmistakable colors	2 Like a coward
3 In skulls and bones	3 With tactical thought
4 In finery	4 To his last breath
5 Barely at all	5 With dazzling grace
6 Like me	6 Like me
Speaks	**Would never**
1 With infuriating decorum	1 Harm an innocent
2 Boorishly	2 Forsake her homeland
3 In a cool growl	3 Admit he is beaten
4 With unshakable confidence	4 Break an oath
5 Like a salesperson	5 Tell more than a half-truth
6 Like me	6 Enter a fair fight

The Taming of the Wolverine

One of the most popular character archetypes in genre fiction is the anti-authority, antisocial loose cannon who is tough as nails, self-reliant, and always cool. It's easy to see why someone would want to bring a character like this into a game. The problem is antisocial characters can be difficult to incorporate into an ensemble story. Having someone pursue an agenda that works against the party is a recipe for disaster. Loner characters work on teams in fiction because writers give them traits that bind them to the rest of the cast. If you want to create a loner, use these exceptions to keep that character part of the party.

✸ **For each loner trait you want to give your character, choose at least one social trait to balance it.**

I DON'T RESPECT AUTHORITY, BUT... (CHECK AT LEAST ONE)

- O I respect (specific party member).
- O My moral code is usually in line with those of my companions.
- O I need to prove my worth.
- O I'll follow a plan others agree to.
- O I could never abandon my friends.
- O I need to be in charge.

I DON'T GET CLOSE TO PEOPLE, BUT... (CHECK AT LEAST ONE)

- O I compulsively mentor anyone younger than me.
- O I secretly want to find a family.
- O I am always trying to rebuild what I lost.
- O I have a deep friendship with (specific party member).
- O I'm always falling in love.
- O I can never leave anyone alone.

continued

I WORK ALONE, BUT... (CHECK AT LEAST ONE)

- I can't stand to see good people get hurt if I don't help.
- My rivalry with (specific party member) draws me in.
- I can't deny (specific party member) knows things I don't.
- My code of honor doesn't allow me to break a promise.
- The mission is more important than anything.
- I'll always take the most convenient option.

I RUN MY MOUTH, BUT... (CHECK AT LEAST ONE)

- It's only because I really care.
- I would die for my companions.
- It's because I am trying to be someone I am not.
- I need an audience for my nonsense.
- I am deeply empathetic, and it destroys me to hurt people.
- It is because I am trying to keep people who are dear to me out of harm's way.

I'M GREEDY AND SELFISH, BUT... (CHECK AT LEAST ONE)

- It's to support people other than myself.
- I prefer getting caught to showing off my skills.
- I'm deeply ashamed of it.
- I'm always giving away what I take.
- I would never steal from a friend.
- It's only so I can have things to impress people.

My Grimoire 28

Every wizard has a spell book, but very few look anything alike. A spell book is a versatile tool, and for many wizards, it is designed to fit specific needs. Pick details to inspire you to answer the prompts and add personality to your spell book.

Look

On the outside every book has a particular feel. Sometimes this is based on where the wizard was taught; sometimes it's built around an image the wizard wants to project. Others just evolve naturally based on the magic they contain.

The two most prominent descriptors for my spell book:

- Grandiose
- Elegant
- Ancient
- Animalistic
- Foreboding
- Worn
- Ethereal
- Utilitarian
- Mysterious
- Captivating

What material is the cover made of? ____________________

What do the pages feel like? ____________________

What feature signals to even lay observers that this is no ordinary tome?

____

____

____

____

____

Properties

Based on your areas of study, your book has picked up a specialized property. Consult your GM when selecting a property.

 **Choose one based on your school:**

ABJURATION

- O The pages of this book resist most spills and accidental damage.
- O The cover is strong enough to repel a shot from a longbow.
- O It occasionally counters cantrips from casters it does not like.

CONJURATION

- O Bookmarks and highlights appear and disappear spontaneously.
- O A usable quill can be pulled from the spine; it disappears after not touching the book for ten minutes.
- O Once per day, a mundane spell component can be found between the seventy-seventh and seventy-eighth pages.

DIVINATION

- O The book will serendipitously store itself in the least vulnerable place among your possessions.
- O Occasionally, new spells appear on the pages in your handwriting before you even master them.
- O With an hour-long ritual, you can fill a page with a detailed account of events that took place within twenty feet up to twenty-four hours ago as though you had written it.

ENCHANTMENT

- O The book can implant the impulse in intelligent creatures to read the ninety-ninth page upon seeing the book laid open.
- O Once per day, with a silent command, the book will emit a smell repulsive to unintelligent creatures.
- O An unauthorized person who touches the book will feel a powerful urge to do something.

EVOCATION

- This book resists damage from an element of your choosing (fire, acid, cold, etc.).
- Tearing a page and expending a spell slot will create a thrown weapon that does damage 1d4/level when it comes in contact with a person or thing.
- Once per day, a minor elemental phenomenon can be trapped between its pages and will be released when the book is opened again.

ILLUSION

- This book appears to be a mundane object unless it is specifically sought after.
- When an unauthorized reader opens the book, certain words jump and swim across the page.
- This book shifts in color and style to suit your mood.

NECROMANCY

- Slapping this book on the chest of a dying ally will grant you advantage on attempts to stabilize him.
- Bothersome insects within ten feet of this book spontaneously drop dead.
- Once per day, you can write a note to a creature in a plane of the dead.

TRANSMUTATION

- A beverage placed on the cover of this book will come to a pleasant drinking temperature within seconds.
- Water that runs along the spine of this book will be safe to drink unless affected by a major curse.
- Tearing a page from this book and expending a spell slot will transform the page into a material of the caster's choice as thick as the page. Exotic materials require higher spell slots.

continued

Personality

Spell books are not alive, but magic is. Grimoires tend to develop quirks and personalities based on the wizards who use them and the spells contained within them.

✸ **Choose one:**

- O This book detests periods of inactivity and deliberately maneuvers itself into precarious positions.
- O This book prefers to be placed on the table during social events and becomes finicky if it feels as if it is missing out.
- O This book prefers you to keep certain company and forces you to interact with certain people.
- O This book detests small animals and will act against them when it can.
- O This book loves music and behaves better during a musical performance.
- O This book is vain and transforms mundane writing in its pages into illuminated text.
- O This book fears the dark and glows when it is in shadow.
- O This book respects strength and resists when someone attempts to turn a page.
- O This book loves peace and resists violent spells written in its pages.
- O This book craves secrets and hides new information from prying eyes.
- O This book loves to teach and will seek potential wizards to instruct.
- O This book holds the soul of an old spellcaster who occasionally speaks to the current holder.

Familiar, but Not Too Familiar 29

Some casters keep a familiar, a living thing created by magic, which assists them in their duties. Unfortunately, familiars have the tendency to disappear in larger stories, and their roles as fun character features get lost along with them. This exercise will help give your familiar a little more personality.

Foundation

Knowing where your familiar came from can help you craft a unique personality for it.

- **Personal:** A familiar may contain aspects of your personality that have been given life. Although it is technically a part of you, it does not have all your inhibitions and careful social graces. You can communicate information about aspects of your personality you normally conceal through the actions of your familiar. You can take this approach even further by interpreting your familiar as aspects of your personality you deliberately removed from yourself and fashioned into a new entity. A familiar may be a greedy coward because, as a brave wizard, you have little use for those feelings.
- **Prisoner:** Your familiar could be an actual person who was imprisoned in an animal shape for a slight he committed against you or someone close to you. In order to earn his freedom, he must serve you for an allotted time. This allows your familiar to be a separate entity with his own motivation. He may not even share your agenda, but he is forced to carry out your commands. He might even be a hostile force or an earnest being looking for redemption.
- **Guardian:** You familiar can be a benevolent entity that has an interest in your success. This might mean she is the servant of a god or a source of secret power who acts as a patron to your journey. She could be the spirit of an ancestor summoned back to the mortal plane to assist you. This allows your familiar to possess knowledge and skill you may not; this in turn can make her a valuable resource at every stage of your story. She may gently try to impose an agenda on you during your journey.

- **Elevated:** Some familiars are animals or objects granted intelligence and power. Their behaviors and desires could be related to what they once were. A cat might crave food and attention and be equipped to seek them out. A teapot might prefer warm environments and have distinct desires for sophisticated table manners. Note that an elevated familiar is never *not* what it appears to be.

Appearance

A familiar should look distinct from other things of its type. It can blend in when it needs to, but it should have a suggestion of importance and mystery that betrays its true nature. This may be something obvious, such as a supernatural glow or unusual anatomy. It may be subtle, like the way it moves, or manifest in behavioral quirks. It should definitely separate the familiar from mundane creatures and objects.

Consider these questions:

Is there something special about its eyes? ....

Does it move in an unnatural way? ....

How do animals interact with it? ....

Are there any unusual markings on its body? ....

Does it bear a visual similarity to you? ....

Is it an unusual size? ....

Does it choose to decorate itself? ....

continued

Desires

A quick path to developing a personality is giving a creature goals. A creature that wants something is compelled to act in order to get it.

SHORT TERM

 **What is always an immediate motivator for your familiar?** It should be something simple like food, alcohol, wealth, or attention.

LONG TERM

 **What is a dream your familiar has?** It should be a little abstract or unusual. It can be tied to its base form, like a raven's desire to possess the world's shiniest bauble. It can also be personal and totally abstract like freedom and independence. It's best if this is something you might want for your familiar but don't know how to get.

SOCIAL

 **What are the social preferences your familiar has?** Social preferences will give your familiar a trait that enables it to interact with others, and that is key for giving it a personality. Perhaps your familiar is a creature of refined taste and prefers the company of nobility. It could be a fun-loving prankster that can't stand stuffy company. A social preference should give a familiar an ideal operating environment, rather than emphasize how it is out of place in other environments.

A Touch of Home

Constantly on the road, most adventurers split their time between staying at inns and camping in dangerous places. Even for the most hardened nomads, an inn can feel sterile and cold without some homey touches. Answer the prompts to discover what your character does to make a strange room feel like home.

During the months when the cold stings even indoors, inns tend to skimp on the sheets.

What do you bring to keep yourself warm?

Although there are hidden gems everywhere, most inns don't pride themselves on culinary delicacies.

What do you always keep with you to liven up a bland meal?

Wood, thatch, pitch, and mud—the materials most inns are built from—are warmer than a tent but aren't exactly pretty.

What colorful thing cuts through the monotony of most inns?

An evening of carousing often leads to singing and swapping stories.

What tale or song do you bring to an evening of revelry to warm your homesick heart?

Not every hero gambles his or her treasure, but almost all adventurers play games to pass the time.

What is your favorite thing to play?

For some adventurers, taking a bath is the ultimate luxury.

When you're not scrubbing away the dirt of the road, how do you make the most of the experience?

Vision of the Future

One of your adventures causes you to come into contact with a future version of yourself. Answer the prompts to craft an image of this bizarre scene.

What lets you know that this strange occurrence is not an illusion?

What about the appearance of your future self fills you with pride or hope?

What about the version's voice, demeanor, or power fills you with uncertainty or dread?

What reason does the figure give you for not answering your most pressing questions?

What is something you have always known that the figure confirms as true?

Your future self delivers a message or warning: (choose two)

- O It has advice that must be followed.
- O It is incredibly specific.
- O It involves an event that will occur distressingly soon.
- O It exposes a masked threat.
- O It requires tremendous courage to bear.
- O It requires secrecy.
- O It gives you a vague but powerful tool.

What did your future self tell you?

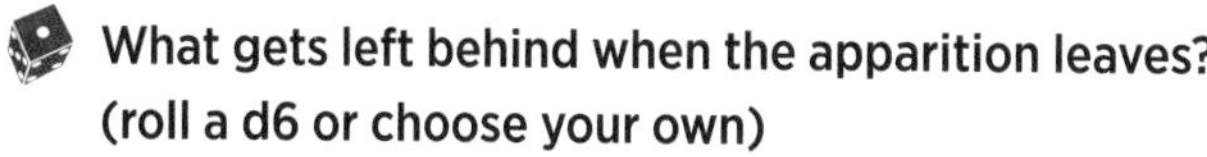

What gets left behind when the apparition leaves? (roll a d6 or choose your own)

1. A body
2. Evidence of your future travel that is strangely familiar
3. A strange object you do not recognize
4. A message or tool in a container you cannot open
5. Something precious to you that has visibly aged
6. Something that belongs to an enemy

Mentor

Create a mentor for your character.

✸ **Select the qualities of your mentor, ensuring that he or she has at least one each in the A, B, C, D, and E categories.**

A. Reputation

- ○ **A Myth:** Your mentor is lauded as a once-in-a-millennium genius. Long after she passes from this world, scholars will study her work, and bards will sing songs of her deeds.
- ○ **Well Respected:** Your mentor is considered one of the world's foremost experts in her field.
- ○ **Known to Some:** Your mentor is recognizable in certain circles, but she is far from a household name.
- ○ **An Oddity:** Most do not know your mentor; those who do consider her work to be far outside the mainstream of her field.
- ○ **Wicked:** Your mentor is rarely spoken of by anyone in her field, but when she is, it is not in kind terms. She is considered incompetent, unsound, dangerous, or some combination of the three.

B. Relationship

- ○ **Favored:** You are never far from your mentor's mind. He believes you to be a chosen one or some kind of generation-defining genius.
- ○ **Star Pupil:** Your mentor remembers you as exceptionally bright and talented. They avidly track your progress and encourage your success.
- ○ **Familiar:** You stood out from the other students your mentor taught, perhaps not always for the right reasons. Were he to see you again, it would take only a short time for him to recall your time together.
- ○ **Disappointment:** For one reason or another, your mentor feels you wasted your potential. They think of you often, not fondly.
- ○ **None:** Your mentor does not remember you.

C. Resources

- O **Master of Unknown:** Your mentor has access to things beyond mortal understanding. She possesses items of legend and easily walks in places of myth.
- O **Wealth Beyond Measure:** Your mentor's wealth rivals that of some kingdoms. All that can be bought with gold is within her reach.
- O **Accomplished:** Your mentor owns a modest property with access to a few comforts and fine materials related to her trade.
- O **Down on Her Luck:** Your mentor struggles with debt and day-to-day expenses. These bring her considerable trouble that she cannot deal with on her own.
- O **Ascetic:** Your mentor places no value on material wealth. She owns nothing and gives away what little she finds.

D. Skill

- O **Holder of Hidden Truths:** Your mentor has walked between worlds and understands things that others could spend thousands of lifetimes failing to comprehend. Any who witness him perform even simple tasks can innately sense they are in the presence of a living myth. At some tasks even gods cannot rival his mastery.
- O **Greatest Alive:** Perhaps there once was or will one day be a talent to rival your master, but among mortal beings, he has no equal. Even with your formal instruction behind you, there is much you could learn from him.
- O **Competent:** Your mentor has undeniable ability. He can teach many, though there are few lessons he now has to teach you.
- O **Those Who Cannot Do:** Due to age, injury, or illness, your mentor has lost some or much of his former prowess. The lessons you have yet to learn are beyond his ability to teach.
- O **Charlatan:** You mentor is not the person you or the world once thought him to be. Though you may have learned much from him, it has nothing to do with his own ability. Perhaps he is practiced in theory, or maybe he just happened to nudge you in ways that unlocked your natural talents.

E. Accessibility

- ○ **With You Always:** Your mentor's guidance is never far from your ear. Perhaps they are an ever-present watchful spirit, or contact is the result of a simple spell. Whatever the circumstance, guidance is there when you need it and absent when this drives you to achieve something on your own.
- ○ **A Call Away:** Your mentor is easy to find and reach. Writing a letter or looking in a particular place will almost always gain you their ear.
- ○ **Rarely Present:** Your mentor is busy or always moving. Without specific knowledge, clever tricks, or considerable effort, it is difficult to establish contact.
- ○ **Wandering Wind:** Your mentor is impossible to find when you need her and the source of many troubles when she is around. It is never convenient or easy to depend on her in any way.
- ○ **Dead:** Your mentor is beyond your reach.

Magic Mirrors

One of the most insidious magical devices is the magic mirror. It whispers lies and truths that beguile heroes and lead them astray. Answer the prompts to discover the insidious visions one might show you.

What desire is so powerful that it could tempt you into idle pining?

What point of pride would you take great pains to defend?

What grim vision could fill you with unknown fear?

What promise could fill you with empty hope?

What personal flaw or failing could fill you with deep shame?

Visualizing Intellect

There is more than one flavor of smart character. Creating a visual guide to your approach to intelligence can help you diversify your playstyle and keep characters feeling fresh.

Manifestation

Not all "smart" people have the same capabilities or approach to intellect. These differences can create vast differences in the way a character behaves and solves problems.

✸ **Choose one of the following based on your most prominent features:**

- ○ **Seeking:** You acquire knowledge by seeking it out through study and scholarship. You are smart because you put the work in to find the truth and know how the world around you works.
- ○ **Understanding:** You can take in information and intuitively make sense of it. You don't need much instruction, and traditional schooling is not worth your time.
- ○ **Deduction:** You solve problems by constructing logical chains of information based on observing your environment.
- ○ **Instinct:** With very little information, you can react to a situation with clarity. You might not have all the details, but you are able to cut out the noise and focus on exactly what you need to act.

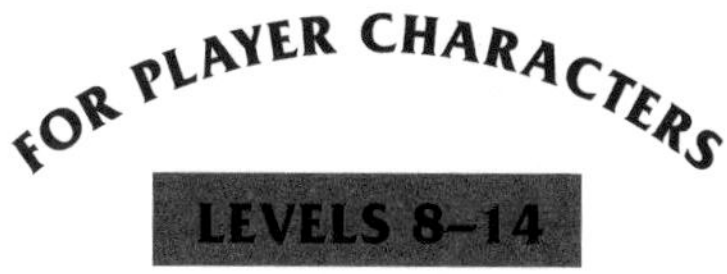

Veteran Heroes

35 Five Scars

Years of adventuring have left physical traces on your body. This exercise will define those scars and help you determine your relationship with your body.

36 Wed, Bed, or Behead

Over a campfire and drinks strong enough to keep out the cold, seasoned adventurers challenge one another with the ultimate question.

37 The One That Got Away

You don't regret your life as a hero, but there is someone in your past who occasionally makes you wonder how things might have gone differently.

38 Never Have I Ever...

You and your party stare in disbelief at the massive obsidian hand that rose from the earth. You can tell by the malevolent glow of the tomb guardian's eyes that unless you play, you will not be allowed to pass. This can be played solo or with the whole group.

39 Last Will

Death is always a possibility in your line of work. How have you prepared yourself in the event that your companions are left with your corpse or your belongings are found by some other party?

40 My Friends

An inventory of the problems your character's companions face and how your character thinks they can be resolved. These questions draw your attention to the stories of other characters to make you invest in a more collaborative narrative.

41 I Know You from *Somewhere*

Your character is approached at a ball by a supremely well-dressed noble. After a few minutes of conversation, you realize you know her, but you can't remember if you helped her or wronged her.

42 Five Things You Can't Throw Away

Answer prompts to discover items that an experienced adventurer can't bring herself to part with.

43 These Things Rarely Work Out

You have a stack of love letters from someone you met on a previous adventure. You wrote less and less, and you never sent your last note.

44 A Traveler's Taste

In each place you visit, you find one local product or delicacy that you look for in other lands. Finding one of these is a tremendous boon.

45 I've Heard Stories about These

When you roll poorly on a check to identify the strange beasts you encounter, you can roll on these tables to invent inaccurate rumors your character may have heard in his or her travels.

46 **Cursed**

Has your character been placed under a curse?

47 **We Clean Up Well**

In order to attend a ball or other formal event, you put together a fancy outfit. How much does it reflect your inner life?

48 **Song of Folly**

You encounter a bard song based on one of your adventures. It explores how an outsider might view your actions.

49 **Old Haunts**

You remember details about a place where you used to live.

50 **Atonement**

Sometimes you do something wrong. How will you make up for it?

51 **Wanted**

A guide to creating a wanted poster for your character or party.

52 **It's More Than Personal**

Generate details about the Big Bad Evil Guy (BBEG) of a campaign to make him even more personally distasteful in your character's eyes.

53 **Movements of a Master**

A look at how your spells and martial techniques have improved, becoming more fluid and practiced over time.

54 **Campfire**

A game that can be played at or away from the table with or without a partner. Guides you through an intimate conversation that reveals secrets about both of you.

55 **Hero's Best Friend**

Creating an animal companion using the priority system: intellect, strength, stealth, senses, loyalty.

56 **Unheard Confession**

Your character is keeping a secret from one or more companions. There are five ways you consciously and unconsciously communicate indirectly.

57 **A Taste of Death**

Adventurers sometimes die and return to life. How does this affect your character?

58 **Conquered Fear**

Your character had five fears before he or she started adventuring. What moments helped him or her conquer these fears?

59 **Getting to Know You**

Pick the party member you and your companions know the least about. Learn ten things about him or her.

60 **A Show of Force**

A drunk challenges you at a local tavern. How do you handle the situation? What is the result?

61 **Five Times Your Name Was Cursed**

A look at people you have bested, swindled, or hurt on your journey.

62 **Mountains and Molehills**

Pick something that was said to you in the last session of your game and have your character stew over it.

63 **Life Goes On**

Take a look at how the fallout from one of your battles slowly creates a new natural order.

64 In the Eye of My Enemy

When someone who knows you well is looking for you, what specific markers does she seek to follow your trail?

65 Irrational Taste

An examination of the rations you choose to pack.

66 Fish Story

Over time and many retellings, one of your accomplishments has slowly transformed into an unbelievable tale of heroism.

67 You Have No Idea

A story generator about a familiar or animal companion that has a difficult time doing a simple thing.

68 The Gauntlet

A checklist of wild wounds and injuries you may have endured as a fantasy protagonist.

69 Honey Pot

Someone constructs the perfect trap for you. What does this person use as bait?

70 Trusty Steed

A priority system approach to detailing the qualities of your mount: speed, courage, strength, mobility, and endurance.

Five Scars

Adventuring leaves a mark on anyone who adopts the lifestyle. Scars create a visual history for heroes. The following prompts describe scars your character might carry. Select details and use them to create scars for her or him.

When you were young, you were injured doing something innocent or routine. You recovered and were left with a mark that has been part of you so long you cannot imagine yourself without it. You have told the story a thousand times with a laugh around campfires, in a whisper between bedsheets, and over a stiff drink in taverns.

Where? Chin, cheek, brow, or ....

It: (choose one)

- O adds charm to your smile
- O makes you look serious
- O hides behind your hair

....

Do you have a nickname for it? ....

When you were studying your current profession, ambition drove you to a challenge you were not prepared for. That day taught you a measure of humility. Occasionally, your fingers run across this mark when you are facing a daunting challenge.

Where? Arm, hands, neck, or ....

You: (choose one)

- O never tried something like that again
- O were more careful on your second attempt
- O found the strength to try again when the moment was right

How many drinks does it take to get you to talk about it? ....

In a confrontation with a hated rival, you suffered a wound that still causes you pain from time to time. Healers told you it did not mend properly. It makes you slower, weaker, and vulnerable to foes who know you well. You have worked hard to compensate for this injury—you may have even conquered it—but the phantom pain and psychological injuries always find a way to return.

Where? Shoulder, knee, eye, or ....

Did you win the fight? Yes/No/Doesn't matter (choose one)

How long did it take to heal? ....

You received this mark from someone you loved and trusted. It may not be physical, and it may not be the result of a wound, but it is a part of who you are, and that is obvious to someone who takes the time to look.

What? Broken heart, tattoo, piercing, or ....

She or he: (choose one)

- O still waits for you to come home
- O wouldn't spit on you to put out a fire
- O must be out there somewhere

Does someone you truly love need to know this story? ....

You don't remember how you got this. When you tell that to some people, it troubles them. Others nod in recognition, for they also bear marks without name or origin. Some healers have told you that it can be removed, but you have yet to find the motivation to go to that trouble over something so small.

Where? Chest, back, thigh, or ....

This mark is: (choose one)

- O crooked and deep
- O an unusual shape
- O not much larger than a fist

Can you see it when you go through your morning routine? ....

Wed, Bed, or Behead

Over a campfire and drinks strong enough to keep out the cold, seasoned adventurers challenge one another with this ultimate question.

This section lists characters so you can choose who you would wed, bed, or behead.

- The lich king
- The spider goddess
- The great dragon tyrant
- The head of the thieves' guild
- The chief of the watch
- The chief justice of the high court
- The world's greatest sword fighter
- The world's most powerful magician
- The world's most talented musician
- The butcher
- The baker
- The candlestick maker
- The lord of vampires
- The mummified king
- The patchwork man
- The wicked witch
- The treacherous vizier
- The wolf
- A half-orc bard
- A gnome barbarian
- The god of love
- The god of wealth
- The god of luck
- The primary antagonist in your game
- Any party member
- The most beloved NPC in your game

The One That Got Away

You don't regret your life as a hero, but there is someone in your past who occasionally makes you wonder how things might have gone differently. Using multiple choice and fill-in-the-blanks, craft an NPC who could have changed your life.

There was once someone in your life who could have led you down a different path. She or he was: (choose one)

- O A lover
- O A mentor
- O A rival

What made this person beautiful?

What made this person strong?

His, her, or their life was...

- O Simple and honest
- O Lavish and sweet
- O Dark and dangerous
- O Patient and rewarding
- O Romantic and exciting

She or he or they asked me only for...

- O Love
- O Loyalty
- O Diligence
- O Passion
- O Faith

This person taught me:

Through that, I learned this, which is something I can never lose:

We were together for...

- O What seems like minutes
- O An intense few months
- O Several sweet years

What called you away?

How long before you left did you tell your companion you were going?

- O Minutes
- O Hours
- O A day
- O A week
- O I never did

What did your friend give you before you left?

Could you face this person again, as you are now?

Never Have I Ever...

You and your party stare in disbelief at the massive obsidian hand that has risen from the earth. You can tell by the malevolent glow of the tomb guardian's eyes that unless you play, you will not be allowed to pass. Play Never Have I Ever with your party; if you have done one of the actions named, lower a finger as a strike. Allow yourself five strikes before you are taken out of the game. Whoever is removed first loses.

- Killed a creature that could not defend itself
- Shared a bed with someone whose name I didn't know
- Fought a battle I could not win
- Stood for a cause I did not believe in
- Been cursed
- Heard the voice of a god
- Lost a great love
- Sought revenge for a wrong done to me
- Witnessed a violent crime
- Talked to an animal
- Fought a vampire
- Kissed someone of noble blood
- Cast a spell
- Held a sword in battle
- Been certain that I was about to die
- Lost a limb
- Been on an adventure before this one
- Had a rival
- Been spared by a stronger opponent
- Lost a parent
- Been betrayed by someone close
- Been fooled by an illusion
- Run from a fight
- Been too late to make a difference
- Been at the mercy of another worldly being

Last Will 39

Death is always a possibility in your line of work. How have you prepared yourself for the possibility that your companions will be left with your corpse? What if your belongings are found by some other party? This exercise will allow you the opportunity to take stock of who and what are important to you in the event of your demise.

How have you used your talents to store your final wishes and keep them safe from forces that might kill you?

To whom or what do you bequeath your wealth (gold, jewels, and general treasure)?

Whom in your party do you trust to see that this request is carried out?

continued

To whom or what do you leave your tools of the trade (weapons, armor, and magical items)?

Do you have anything that you need to say to each of your companions in a final message? Perhaps words you do not have the strength to say in life?

Is there a quest you must leave to your party? A task that you live for and believe it capable of taking on in your absence?

What if you are found not by your companions but by a stranger? What message would you have for a fellow wanderer on the road? Would you ask her or him to perform a duty?

My Friends 40

One of the greatest gifts players can give each other is to buy into each other's character stories. It's easy to get wrapped up in your own narrative, but finding a place for yourself in a companion's story makes both characters more dynamic and fun to play. This exercise will help you chart another character's story so you can find ways to interact with it.

Companion's name: ...., the:

- O Kindest
- O Wisest
- O Most formidable
- O Most resourceful
- O Cleverest
- O Most tragic
- O Bravest

person I have ever met.

Where are he, she, or they from?

Where did the character learn his, her, or their skills?

Why is she or he traveling with you?

What is the drive for the character's quest?

- O Intellectual
- O Emotional
- O Spiritual

continued

What five things does the character need to complete the quest that she, he, or they lack now?

1. ____________________
2. ____________________
3. ____________________
4. ____________________
5. ____________________

What three talents do you have that your friend lacks?

1. ____________________
2. ____________________
3. ____________________

Which of your talents is best suited to getting the character one of the things she or he needs to complete this quest?

____

Why does your character care about this?

____

What is your plan to further this mission next session?

____

What can you do to counsel the character through the tasks you cannot aid?

____

I Know You from *Somewhere*

This exercise will take you on a simulated adventure that you can play through using a character from a D&D game. Occasionally it will ask you to make skill and ability checks at a certain "Difficulty Class," or DC. That means you have to add your ability modifier or skill bonus to a d20 roll. If the total of your bonus and roll is higher than the DC, you succeed.

You are a guest at a ball for powerful nobility. You are approached by a well-dressed noblewoman with a predatory look in her eye. She looks familiar, but you can't place her. She greets you by name and remarks, "It is nice to see you again," with a cool smile.

- O To try to remember: ⟶ section 1
- O To take action: ⟶ section 2
- O To search her appearance and manner for clues: ⟶ section 3

1 Roll a d6 to search your memory.

  - 1 ⟶ section 1.1
  - 2-5 ⟶ section 1.2
  - 6 ⟶ section 1.3

1.1 You have *no* idea who this could be. ⟶ section 2.2

1.2 This could be the eldest daughter of a noble house you *may* have crossed when you borrowed its prize jewel to open an ancient tomb. Or it's one of your enemies disguised as a noblewoman, come to spy on you.

- O To issue a veiled threat: ⟶ section 1.2.1
- O To pass her false information: ⟶ section 1.2.2

1.2.1 Roll a DC 14 Intimidation to scare her off.

Failure: ⟶ section 1.2.1.1

Success: ⟶ section 1.2.1.2

1.2.1.1 She smiles wickedly and tells you to enjoy your drink. ⟶ section 2.1

1.2.1.2 Her face grows pale, and she leaves you alone for the rest of the evening.

1.2.2 Roll a DC 16 Deception to throw her off your trail.
Failure: ⟶ section 1.2.2.1
Success: ⟶ section 1.2.2.2

1.2.2.1 She rolls her eyes and leaves you alone. After a few drinks you step out to get some fresh air. Take Disadvantage on your next check. ⟶ section 2.2

1.2.2.2 You confide in her that you are working with the watch to entrap an old enemy. You ask her to keep her eyes peeled for a duplicitous scoundrel in gaudy dress, as that person will be brought up on charges of corruption and criminal conspiracy. She grows quiet, then pale, then excuses herself. You enjoy the rest of your ball. **THE END**

1.3 This is the unfortunate-looking crown princess, who has a bad reputation because she looks less trustworthy than she is. You try to curry favor. Roll a DC 12 Charm.
Failure: ⟶ section 1.3.1
Success: ⟶ section 1.3.2

1.3.1 You do manage to charm her; she's just a profound bore. Your evening is wasted on an overly complex discussion of tax codes. **THE END**

1.3.2 You have managed to win her over. After a pleasant conversation, she asks your advice on a difficult matter of state. Make a DC 14 Wisdom or Intelligence check.
Failure: ⟶ section 1.3.2.1
Success: ⟶ section 1.3.2.2

1.3.2.1 She politely thanks you for your time. You enjoy your evening. **THE END**

1.3.2.2 You have solved a difficult problem. She confides a title to you and offers you a reward. **THE END**

2 Unable to identify this person after a short conversation, you decide you have to act. Roll a d6.

1-2 → section 2.1
3-5 → section 2.2
6 → section 2.3

2.1 You try to move out of the room only to find yourself growing dizzy. It's too late to slow the poison already in your system. You collapse, and her wicked smile is the last thing you see. **THE END**

2.2 You make your way to the back door to find a band of hired thugs waiting for you. Make a DC 15 Constitution save.

Failure: → section 2.2.1

Success: → section 2.2.2

2.2.1 You are severely beaten and robbed of all valuables you were carrying. You will not look back on this night fondly. **THE END**

2.2.2 Take 53 damage, expend any long rest combat powers, and four spell slots of your highest level. You limp around the estate to your waiting carriage and climb in. → section 3.3.1

2.3 You deftly weave your way through the room, moving between partygoers in similar dress. Make a DC 16 Stealth check to ensure your exit.

Failure: → section 2.3.1

Success: → section 2.3.2

2.3.1 Despite your careful movement, you can tell you have been marked. → section 2.2.2 but subtract 10 from the damage you will take.

2.3.2 You exit the building and manage to slip past an unfriendly band of mercenaries waiting outside. You hop into a carriage to make your escape. → section 3.3.1

3 You reach for a familiar symbol or crest you can use to identify this person. Roll a d6.

1-3 ⟶ section 3.1
4-5 ⟶ section 3.2
6 ⟶ section 3.3

3.1 You see around her neck a cluster of black pearls, a hidden sign of the assassin's guild. You cover your surprise by sipping your drink only to taste the subtle notes of poison in your wine. You know assassins carry antidote with them. You must act quickly and carefully. Make a DC 15 Sleight of Hand check.

Failure: ⟶ section 3.1.1
Success: ⟶ section 3.1.2

3.1.1 Trying to remain calm, you offer a dance and use the opportunity to reach into her handbag. You retrieve a small bottle. After the dance ends you examine your prize, only to find it contains a note that reads, "Too late." You grow dizzy. Make a DC 16 Constitution save.

Failure: ⟶ section 3.1.1.1
Success: ⟶ section 3.1.1.2

3.1.1.1 Your vision swims as you begin to pass out. You see other guests begin to sway and fall as wicked laughter fills the air. **THE END**

3.1.1.2 You pass out and awaken to find yourself in a ballroom surrounded by dead guests. Take 45 damage; any possessions you were carrying, including weapons, are now missing. You unsteadily move to escape, but you must choose to exit through the back or front.

Back: ⟶ section 3.1.2.2
Front: ⟶ section 3.1.2.1

3.1.2 You skillfully slip the necklace from her neck. The dance ends, and you slip away. You bite into a single white pearl on the necklace and taste the bitter antidote hidden inside. As people collapse around you and the room fills with screams, you hurry for an exit.

- Head out the back: ⟶ section 3.1.2.2
- Head out the front: ⟶ section 3.1.2.1

3.1.2.1 Head to the front entrance: you see your carriage and hop on. ⟶ section 3.3.1

3.1.2.2 Head to the back: you make your way to the back door. ⟶ section 2.2

3.2 On her hand is a ring with a truly dazzling sapphire.

Make a DC 15 Investigation or history roll to identify it.

Failure: ⟶ section 3.2.1

Success: ⟶ section 3.2.2

3.2.1 You puzzle over it for some time but cannot recall its significance. You compliment the gem, winning you a bashful smile. She offers her ring to kiss, as is customary in this region. The evening goes on, and eventually you must leave. Do you go out the back or front?

- Head out the back: ⟶ section 3.1.2.2
- Head out the front: ⟶ section 3.1.2.1

3.2.2 This is the maiden's tear, an infamous cursed object. Any who touch it are sure to suffer a grisly fate. She sees you notice her ring and offers to let you kiss it, as is customary in this region.

- Kiss the ring: ⟶ section 3.2.2.2
- Try and get out of it: ⟶ section 3.2.2.3

3.2.2.2 You kiss her ring and pray for protection.

Make a DC 16 Religion check.

Failure: ⟶ section 3.2.2.2.1

Success: ⟶ section 3.2.2.2.2

continued

3.2.2.2.1 The world around you begins to swim and fade. You hear screams. ⟶ section 3.1.1.2

3.2.2.2.2 Faced with the power of your faith, the darkness within the ring fades. You see the expression on the young woman's face change, and she utters a breathless "Thank you" before fading away. You spend the rest of your evening avoiding drink. **THE END**

3.2.2.3 You try to talk your way out of touching that awful thing. Make a DC 15 Persuasion check.

Failure: ⟶ section 3.2.2.3.1

Success: ⟶ section 3.2.2.3.2

3.2.2.3.1 Her eyes darken, and you can feel the hatred emanating from her as she walks away. **THE END**

3.2.2.3.2 You refuse, saying that your lips are not worthy of such a fine gem. She laughs and walks away. You enjoy a quiet evening. **THE END**

3.3 This is one of your most hated enemies in a very bad disguise. You see which direction the wind is blowing and excuse yourself. You immediately go through the front entrance and jump into your carriage.

⟶ section 3.3.1

3.3.1 You race away from the party, hoping to put this evening behind you. About a mile down the road some shadowy figures block your path. They shout for you to stop. You must choose:

- O Stop and face them: ⟶ section 3.3.1.1
- O Subtly draw a weapon (if you have one): ⟶ section 3.3.1.3
- O Cast a spell: ⟶ section 3.3.1.2
- O Reveal the necklace (if you found one): ⟶ section 3.3.1.4

3.3.1.1 Stop and fight. Your opponents are strong and skilled. It is a brutal and bloody battle. You lose 60 HP. If you survived, you managed to escape. **THE END**

3.3.1.2 Choose your highest available spell slot and subtract 10 damage for each level. ⟶ section 3.3.1.1

3.3.1.3 If you have a weapon, subtract 10 damage from the ensuing battle. ⟶ section 3.3.1.1

3.3.1.4 Reveal the necklace you stole. The figures in the road recognize it as a sign of the assassins guild. They stand aside and allow you to pass. **THE END**

42 Five Things You Can't Throw Away

Surviving the life of an adventurer is difficult. It takes discipline and sacrifice. That should never compromise a character's individualism. Even the most road-worn heroes hang on to things they shouldn't. Answer the prompts to discover items that an experienced adventurer like you refuses to part with despite knowing better.

Found in a Dungeon

You have been holding on to something no larger than your fist. Long ago, you found it in a dungeon. At first you saved it because you thought it might be useful, but you never found its purpose.

What about its shape makes it unusual? What would you want it to do?

Given As a Gift

You received a piece of fine clothing that you have only had occasion to wear once or twice. It is well tailored and far too fine to discard, but it takes up needed space in your pack.

What sort of clothing is it? Who gave it to you?

Won As a Prize

You have a small scrap of cloth or metal that you kept after a difficult fight against one of your earliest adversaries. Perhaps the memory of your enemy and his or her motivations has faded, but the fight itself is clear.

What clever trick or talent did you use to best your foe? Do you still pause when you come across this trophy when rustling through your pack?

Taken from Home

This item bears your strongest connection to the last place you called home. It may not be the memento you originally took with you. In fact it could be something you picked up in an unrelated place. It's bulky, and you rarely need it.

Did it ever get damaged? How would you deal with that?

Holding Temporarily

Years ago, you agreed to give something to someone you know well who is now all but totally beyond your reach. Discarding it would be admitting that your last connection has been severed.

What is your relationship to this person? What emotion do you feel when you think of her or him?

These Things Rarely Work Out

You have a stack of love letters from someone you met on a previous adventure.

Answer the prompts to learn about this relationship and yourself.

Where do you keep them? --

What makes them distinct from your other correspondence?

When is the last time you received one? --

How many have you received? --

How many have you sent? --

What promise did you make to each other?

How often do you think about this person these days?

You have not sent your next letter yet. Why?

What part of your letter do you erase and rewrite constantly?

If you saw this person again, could you look her or him in the eye?

A Traveler's Taste

For each place you visit, you've found one local product or delicacy that you look for in other lands. Finding one of these is a tremendous boon. Pick details and answer the prompts to create hard-to-find treats that occasionally tempt you.

Something Sweet

It doesn't cost much, but it is hard to come across. When you do discover it, you buy all you can carry.

It's... (choose one)

- O A fruit
- O A confection
- O A spice

You recognize it anywhere by... (choose one)

- O Its vibrant color
- O The unusual design on its wrapping
- O Something left over whenever it is eaten
- O A flag the peddlers carry on their carts

Who introduced it to you?

Something Strong

It's expensive even in the place it came from, but a drink like this is worth a little indulgence.

It's... (choose one)

- O A spirit
- O Brewed from something roasted
- O A sort of tea

✸ **It creates a feeling of... (choose one)**

- O Bubbly happiness
- O Deep focus
- O Relaxed serenity
- O Welcome slumber

✎ **What might this drink make better?**

Something Soft

Only the wealthiest people can afford this material. You dream of owning something made from it.

✸ **It's... (choose one)**

- O An animal skin
- O A fleece
- O Something woven from fibers

✸ **It has an amazing property... (choose one)**

- O Under certain conditions, it is lighter than air.
- O It is stronger than steel.
- O It can quickly seal a wound.
- O A small piece can stretch farther than any rope you own

✎ **When did you first touch it?**

I've Heard Stories about These

Characters don't always have the same information players do. Sometimes it's more fun when you don't have all the answers.

When you roll poorly on a check to identify the strange beasts you encounter, you can roll a d6 and consult these tables to invent inaccurate rumors your character may have picked up in his or her travels.

Abilities	Aggressions
1 It can see in darkness	1 Always hunts in packs
2 It breathes fire	2 Naturally docile and never attacks
3 It can turn enemies to stone	3 Deeply aggressive at all times
4 It controls illusions	4 Never attacks unless protecting young
5 It is more intelligent than humanoids	5 Never harms a creature pure of heart
6 It is faster than any horse	6 Able to smell fear

Weaknesses	Defenses
1 Will not cross a line of salt	1 Immune to an element
2 Compulsively counts mustard seeds	2 Resistant to an element
3 Recoils from sunlight	3 Resistant to weapons
4 Vulnerable to an element	4 Regenerates from injury
5 Fears holy objects	5 Nurtured by death
6 Obeys someone who knows its name	6 Can never truly die

continued

Behaviors	Oddities
1 Protects the purity of chaste creatures	1 This creature changes sex under certain conditions
2 Nests once a decade	2 It collects attractive twigs to find mates
3 Makes and delivers toys to children	3 It will drop limbs to confuse predators
4 Buries treasure in the places it hunts	4 It sings songs to entice prey
5 Speaks with trees to find prey	5 It learns a victim's true name when it tastes his or her blood
6 Respects noble titles	6 It dies and is reborn

YOU LEARNED THIS...

1 From an old bestiary
2 From an adventurer who traveled the world
3 From your mentor
4 From your parent
5 From an old story
6 Through "logical" deduction

Cursed

Whether you know it or not, you have been placed under a curse.

Roll a d6 to determine different aspects of this curse and how you'll have to deal with it.

HOW DID YOU ACQUIRE THIS CURSE?

1. You angered a witch.
2. You crossed a vengeful ghost.
3. You offended a petty god.
4. You touched a hexed item.
5. You accidentally desecrated a sacred thing.
6. You failed to observe a common superstition.

IT CAUSES…

1. A mundane piece of equipment you depend on to break constantly.
2. Your hair and nails to grow at an inconveniently accelerated rate.
3. You to compulsively tell the truth when you would prefer to lie.
4. You to see an unsettling figure that is always watching you.
5. You to hear your name in any sentence in which it might offend you.
6. Every drink you touch to eventually spill.

To get rid of it you must… (roll a d6 twice to find your solution or choose two)

1–2
1. Pass it on to another host 2. Kiss someone you have strong feelings for 3. Build a temple 4. Climb a mountain 5. Travel a hundred miles 6. Die and return from death

continued

3–4
1 Do three good deeds
2 Learn a lesson about a friend
3 Grow a particular plant from a seed
4 Sacrifice an animal
5 Construct an apologetic shrine
6 Tend a flame for three days
5–6
1 Bathe in a pure pool
2 Meditate in total darkness
3 Admit you are wrong
4 Throw three round stones into a pond
5 Make an apology
6 Keep a promise

THE WORST ASPECT OF THIS CURSE IS...

1 It's contagious.
2 Something explodes when you try to explain it.
3 It grows stronger with the full moon.
4 It attracts bothersome animals.
5 It covers your skin in strange symbols.
6 You recently made a large wager that you would never fall victim to a curse.

We Clean Up Well

In order to attend a ball or other formal event, your character must dress in formal attire. These prompts will help you find an appropriate and flattering outfit to match your character's personality.

Basic Style

What is the basic style of this outfit?

- Suit: A multipiece ensemble involving trousers and a jacket
- Dress: Usually a single-piece garment that hangs from the upper body
- Robe: A flowing garment that usually covers the wearer's arms and legs
- Uniform: A garment inspired by a profession or military rank
- Unique: An outfit that defies traditional definition but commands elegance

Choose two colors that complement your character's skin and hair to be the primary focus of the ensemble.

For accents, choose at least one color that complements your character's eyes.

What Does the Outfit Convey?

What should it tell people who see you? (choose two)

- I am beautiful.
- I am powerful.
- I am charming.
- I am dangerous.
- I am wise.
- I am just.
- I don't care about any of this.
- I am frightening.

continued

How Does It Move?

Pick a striking facet of your outfit that emphasizes your movement. It could be the way the fabric drapes and flows, how certain details catch the light, or even a magical property that moves with you.

How Does It Shine?

Pick something on your outfit to catch the light. It could be jewelry or stones on your fascinator, or your whole outfit might sparkle.

How Do You Accessorize?

Pick a small item such as a scarf, a hat, a cape, or even a weapon that accompanies the outfit.

How Is It Yours?

Not every character is at ease in formal settings. Some abhor all forms of formal attire. Even so, there is something about this outfit that distinctly matches your personality. It could be related to your class, a reference to your deeds and struggles, or an expression of a theme that captures your essence.

How Are You Prepared?

Few people attend formal events anticipating combat, but in your line of work, these things can happen. Keeping in mind that some venues ban openly carried weapons, how is this outfit going to help you in a fight?

Song of Folly

Sometimes your past catches up with you in unusual places. This exercise explores a bard song based on one of your adventures. Make selections and roll dice to see how an uncomfortable evening plays out.

You and your party wearily enter a tavern and settle in for a well-earned rest. This town is a common stop for travelers, as it is situated between two major settlements. You are surrounded by a wide range of individuals. Fortune-seeking mercenaries, religious pilgrims, peddlers, and common folk fill the air with a din of jovial chatter.

As your drinks and food are served, the sweet tones of an instrument cuts through the noise, and a bard begins her song.

✸ **The tune: (choose one)**

- O Thumps with a beat that heralds an epic tale
- O Whines with a mournful melody
- O Bounces with farcical joy

As the bard runs through her introduction, the crowd falls to mumbles and whispers—the closest a tavern like this gets to rapt attention. Feeling she has the ears of the room, the bard begins to sing. Your road-weary mind relaxes into the tune; the bard sings of a band of adventurers:

✸ **(choose one)**

- O With full hearts and empty heads
- O Bold and foolish
- O Proud and possessed of foul greed
- O Hungry as wolves in a world of sheep

The song is set in a place your party knows well, for it was the staging ground for one of your group's first adventures. Visions flood your mind as the bard expertly paints a picture of the past. The music fades into the background as your comrades whisper recollections to one another, but a few details catch in your mind and pull you from the nostalgic haze. The description of the caster is suspiciously close to one of your companions. You laugh and nudge as he blushes.

The characters in the song continue to match your group, one by one. Though you are never named, the details are uncanny. The least attentive member of your group grins in anticipation of a song based on her heroics, but there is something wrong:

(roll a d6 or choose)

1 The characters were introduced by their flaws.
2 The group is referred to as "the butchers."
3 The tavern occupants laugh where they should gasp.
4 The story is missing important context.
5 One of your enemies was introduced with a heroic chord.
6 The bard has encouraged the crowd to boo.

The rogues in the tale walk the same path as you and your friends, leaving a trail of misery and destruction in their wake. Your table is now full of angry whispers and glowering looks. Hapless, you look to the crowd. Most are caught up in the performance. You grudgingly concede that the song is well sung.

You catch the eye of a ranger who you realize has been staring in your direction.

You: (roll a d6 or choose)

1 Wave meekly
2 Gulp with fear
3 Pointedly turn your attention to your drink
4 Shake your head pleadingly
5 Smirk and wink
6 Quickly discover the ranger is not the only one looking in your direction

Your group quietly decides to find another place to spend the night or perhaps even to get an early start on the next day's journey. As silently as you can, you make your way to the tavern's entrance.

Roll a d6 for your fate:

- **1–2** Just as the song reaches a silent moment, one of you knocks over a bottle of wine, turning the room's full attention to you.
- **3–5** You disappear into the night, unable to shake the tune from your mind.
- **6** You close the door behind you. This causes a lantern to fall from the wall, setting a table ablaze, disrupting the finale of the performance.

As your companions laugh and bicker, you ride in thoughtful silence.

49 Old Haunts

Returning to a place your character used to call home can be a great story line. Often our characters know more about these places than we do. This exercise helps you make the most of a trip back home by filling in details and providing you with options for play. Answer these prompts to bring your past into the present.

General

Choose some large details that strike your character immediately upon their return.

What about this place never changes? Pick a physical detail about this place that transports your character back to their time here. It can be as large as a building or as small as a scratch on a door.

What is different? This place has changed in a way that makes it feel alien. It can be physical or social, but it prevents your character from feeling totally at ease.

Assets

In your former home, you know where to get one of the following essential things: (choose one)

- O Food
- O A safe place to stay
- O Information

Although this thing is easy for you to find, it carries a price: (choose two)

- O It alerts people you are trying to avoid to your presence.
- O It can only be exploited once.
- O It puts someone you care about at risk.
- O It costs you a favor.
- O It is below your usual standard.
- O It reveals something hidden to your companions.

Contacts

A good contact can do something valuable while also complicating a situation. Choose a characteristic in each category to create an NPC who gives and takes at the same time.

I KNOW SOMEONE WHO...	AND HE/SHE...	IT JUST SO HAPPENS HE/SHE...
O Has political authority	O Practically runs this town	O Owes me a favor
O Works in the church	O Has fallen on hard times	O Is related to me
O Possesses secret knowledge	O Is almost universally loathed	O Thinks I'm dead

With that in mind, who is this person?

What is the most physically distinct thing about them?

---

continued

Dangers

✸ **Of course as an adventurer, pretty much everything you do carries risk. Your former home is dangerous because: (choose one)**

- O You used to be involved with a powerful group that doesn't like deserters.
- O You have unsettled debts.
- O Your family wants something from you that you can't surrender.
- O You are technically still on the run from the law.

Atonement

Even heroes do things they regret. Often what separates a true hero from everyone else is how they respond to it. Telling a meaningful redemption story can be difficult. The last thing you want is to waste an awesome dark tragedy on a story not suited to it. This exercise will help you determine the cause of your misdeeds and chart your path to absolution.

Failure

Failure is considered by many gods to be the least serious type of sin. Inability to do right out of weakness, ignorance, or foolishness does not carry the same weight as actively doing evil. The consequences of action remain, so atonement is necessary.

1. **Understand:** To atone, you must first understand the full scope of your deeds. Confront the truth of your actions. Do not turn away from ugly or painful facts. Knowledge will give you the tools you need to overcome failure and perhaps prevent you from walking a similar path in the future.
2. **Ease Suffering:** In most cases a failure cannot be reversed or erased. A person guilty of failure must take steps to ease the suffering he, she, or they has caused. The character is not responsible for setting all the world right but must contribute to a larger effort where possible.
3. **Teach:** Finally, you must take what you have learned and use it to save others from your fate. A failure that prevents another failure has achieved some good.

Various gods and moral judges have different criteria for each of these steps. Some require an extra step of punishment, but that is mostly ceremonial.

continued

Passion

Some misdeeds are the result of desperation or extraordinary circumstances that push mortal beings past limits they normally hold sacred. A starving peasant might steal bread, a frightened parent might kill an intruder to save his child, a person possessed with rage might strike her employer. These are crimes with understandable motivation, even to gods. A sin is still a sin, and a sin of passion is more serious than a sin of failure because it can be prevented.

1. **Admit:** Many who commit misdeeds out of passion try to mask the act with justification. Stricter gods consider this a deeper sin since it allows evil to masquerade as good. An act can be both justified and abhorrent. Atonement can only be found if sin is admitted.
2. **Understand:** Once again, you must understand the consequences of your actions, but in this case, you must also work to understand your motivation. Some acts of passion are driven by powerful needs, others by strong emotion. The same act can have varying degrees of severity. For instance, many think that injuring a person out of rage is a worse crime than taking a life for survival. Careful introspection is required to pass this step.
3. **Penance:** This is a step about which many gods disagree. Some demand suffering in retribution; others ask for good deeds to counter the bad. The cost of penance is tied to the magnitude of the crime. A god who believes a hero has reached understanding will often provide a path to penance.
4. **Forgiveness:** Finally, forgiveness needs to be requested and granted, not only from the wronged party (which can include a deity) but also from oneself.

Some sins of passion are small and easy to forgive; others weigh on souls well into the afterlife. It is not necessary to heed the words of a deity when seeking to atone, but many find clearly defined standards helpful in extraordinary circumstances.

Will

Crimes of will are considered the most grievous and unforgivable acts a mortal being can commit. To commit an act of ill will is to fully comprehend evil and embrace it. A soul who has embraced wickedness through will is in true peril. Most fallen paladins are stripped of their power if they commit evil through an act of will. The road to redemption for sins of will can be long and painful.

1. **Lamentation:** A creature seeking to redeem a sin caused by will must regret its actions on a profound level. For many gods this necessitates a period of punishment or suffering.
2. **Empathy:** Next, you must come to empathize with the being you have wronged. This means you must know that being's suffering and treat it as seriously as you would your own. It is almost impossible for someone to do this without directly confronting his or her victims and accepting mortal punishment for his or her crimes.
3. **Epiphany:** Atoning for acts of will requires a fundamental change to the character's moral framework. It is impossible to pass this step without profound introspection, and very few are capable of doing it alone.
4. **Sacrifice:** To complete atonement for an act of will, you must make a conscious and meaningful sacrifice fitting the scope of your misdeed. Even those who manage to complete epiphany stumble here. Hollow gestures will never tip the cosmic scales. A true sacrifice is a rare opportunity, and it takes true wisdom to recognize the right moment when it comes.

Very few ever redeem major acts of foul will. For some it will take a lifetime.

Wanted

Running into an unexpected wanted poster is a nightmare for some adventurers and a point of pride for others. Make choices and answer the following prompts to craft one for your group to enjoy or lament.

What language is it most likely to be printed in?

- O Common
- O Elvish
- O Dwarfish
- O Goblin
- O Draconic
- O Infernal

Choose at least one crime an outsider might claim your party is guilty of:

- O Murder
- O Breaking and entering
- O Theft
- O Grand theft
- O Arson
- O Vandalism
- O Breach of contract
- O Fraud
- O Identity theft

The poster lists each member of your party with a title or nickname. Choose one for each member of your party:

- O Babyface
- O Mountain Carver
- O The Baron
- O Flame Speaker
- O The Unbreakable
- O Fancy Shoes
- O Silver Tongue
- O Shadowborn
- O The Lesser
- O Loudmouth
- O Big Chief
- O Bones
- O Hot Lips
- O Wildcard
- O Jaws
- O Moonface
- O Iron Heart
- O ---------------------- Slayer
- O Two-Knife
- O Wizard of Odds
- O The Barber
- O The Lethal Ballerina
- O Hot Pipes
- O Bagel Boy
- O Tats
- O Pig Smell
- O The Rat
- O Owlbear
- O Old Man/Old Lady
- O The Clown

This group is considered: (choose two)

- O Armed
- O Dangerous
- O Heretical
- O Seditious
- O Treasonous
- O A threat to the public

To generate a reward, multiply the average level of your party by one thousand and add one hundred gold for each member.

It's More Than Personal

Too often, a GM will introduce the primary antagonist to a game only to find that the adventuring party is less than enthusiastic about opposing her, him, them, or it. The desire to face a truly compelling adversary is understandable, but your GM doesn't have to be alone in making that work. A good villain needs power to be compelling. You can work with the GM to make the big bad of your game as personally offensive as possible.

 **Answer these prompts to fill in details that will create your greatest enemy.**

What about the antagonist do you find frightening or repulsive?
A good villain can offend with his mere presence. This should be something that is almost unignorable once a villain has revealed his true nature. Fear and disgust are powerful emotions; they force you to act in ways you would not when encountering lesser foes.

How does he offend you?
The idea of offense goes beyond being slighted. Something about the villain's behavior or intent should violate part of your core philosophy of right and wrong. You should not be able to coexist with this being.

What has he done to you?

As a hero, it is common to have enemies who try to seriously hurt or injure you. This question refers to a special, premeditated cruelty. Either the villain took time to know you in order to harm you or he is tied to a significant event in your past.

How are you vulnerable?

To make your relationship with a villain meaningful, you must acknowledge him as a threat. The answer to this can be as simple as, "I know I cannot defeat him alone," but it is better to recognize other ways in which you are susceptible to attack.

What will you get if you defeat him?

Finally, there must be a personal motivation to see the villain's end, one that extends beyond your survival, prosperity, or moral conviction. Your reason for wanting to confront him should be distinct from your reason for facing most enemies.

Movements of a Master

Character sheets track your progress. They tell a story of unsteady movements becoming practiced and graceful. Pick one of your spells or abilities and then:

Roll on the chart to prompt a start and an end point for your training.

	At first...		Now, I...
1	I was uncoordinated	1	Possess grace
2	I lacked confidence	2	Move with flair
3	I lacked control	3	Am indomitable
4	I could not understand	4	Carry secrets
5	I was impatient	5	Must be cautious
6	I was weak	6	Have precision

Answer the prompts to chart your story.

Where did you first learn this technique?

When was the first time you had to use it in a high-stakes situation?

What moment provided you with a new level of clarity?

What does it look like when you do it now?

Campfire

You can play this game with a partner at or away from the gaming table. It is designed to structure intimate moments between characters. Ideally, these moments happen around a campfire on a lonely watch, but they can occur in any context in which two characters can speak privately without being interrupted. To play, grab a partner and follow these steps.

Set the Scene

Describe an environment where it is possible for two people to speak openly. Focus on details that make it safe and private. Place your characters in that environment so that they are close enough to understand anything said aloud meant only for their ears. Once you have a setting, introduce your characters. This introduction should be simple, starting with their names, followed by the way the world sees them (race and class are fine for this) and what they believe their missions are. For example:

- Calavar, an Elvish paladin who seeks peace
- Melinda, a halfling bard who brings happiness with music
- Sonya, a human rogue who wants to get away from her past
- Ruga, a half-orc barbarian who wants to test his strength

You can construct your own environment using this form:

A fire burns low under a sky bright with stars. The night is cold, and the world of the earth is dark and still. Two adventurers sit close to keep warm and idly watch shadows that promise no dangers. One is

...., *a* ....

who .... *The other is* ....,

a ...., *who* ....

Tonight, they have no company but each other.

Initiation

One player rolls a d6 to determine what to do to break the silence. You should perform this action in character. Once you have finished, tap the die against the table to signify your action is complete.

1. **Ask an open-ended question:** This is a question that cannot be answered with a simple *yes* or *no*.
2. **Make a confession:** This can be something positive or negative. It does not have to concern the character you are talking to at the moment. It can even be a confession to something obvious that you are putting into words for the first time.
3. **State a fear:** This can be any fear, big or small, so long as it's something that causes you genuine concern.
4. **Ask for help:** This can be for a small problem that can be solved immediately or a large, abstract concern that could take months or years to attend to. It might even be a request for help with something that isn't a problem, like learning a new skill.
5. **Express regret:** While it is good to pick a regret involving the other character, revealing any regret is fine.
6. **Name a desire:** This should be a desire for something that cannot be immediately or obviously fulfilled.

Reaction and Conversation

Now the other player must have her or his character respond by directly addressing what was said. This is not a time to ignore a larger issue out of a desire for stability or comfort. Both characters have to be here in this moment. This does not mean you have to answer any questions asked, but it does mean you need to acknowledge that you heard and understood what was said. If you need guidance, choose one of the suggestions that best suits the moment.

continued

✸ React by:

- **Expressing an emotion:** You can state your feelings or describe a more elaborate emotional reaction without your character actually speaking.
- **Being open:** Allow your barriers to come down and share parts of yourself that you normally hide. It does not mean you have to confess all your secrets, but it exposes a more honest version of yourself.
- **Empathizing:** Extend understanding and care to someone in a vulnerable position. Even if you know you cannot help, honestly identify with that position and look for a way to see him or her outside yourself.

Don't choose a reaction that closes off discussion or shortens the conversation. These two characters have nowhere to be for a while. The alternative to having this discussion is sitting in silence. Encourage the characters to talk through what happened until neither has any more to say.

Once you reach a moment when the conversation hangs on three seconds of silence, either player may end the scene by picking up the die. The player with the die will describe a detail in the environment that reflects an element of the conversation that took place. It can be very small and should be the kind of thing on which a camera might linger after a similar conversation in a movie.

Sharing

Once finished with the environmental detail, the player holding the die will roll it to determine what the characters share at the end of their conversation.

Roll a d6 to determine what will underscore the connection formed between the characters during their conversation:

1. **A drink:** One character will take out something to drink and pass it to the other. If the two just argued, this is an apology that will allow them to continue working together. If their conversation was wholly positive, it shows care and respect.
2. **A look:** This is a moment of eye contact, long or short—a moment when both characters acknowledge what just took place and come to peace with it.
3. **A gesture:** This is a physical interaction between characters. A hug, a kiss, a handshake, or a pat on the shoulder works well as a gesture.
4. **Space:** One character should offer the other the opportunity to get physically closer. This symbolizes the gap between them shrinking.
5. **A promise:** A verbal promise between the characters. It does not have to be one the characters decide to keep long term, but it should be one that they genuinely mean to keep in the moment.
6. **An understanding:** The players will work together to determine what one thing both characters agree on after their conversation. There can still be miscommunication between the two, but they both agree on this fact.

If both players feel there is more they would like to discuss, they can describe an aspect of the environment to suggest the passage of time and go back to initiation. As you play through again, reverse roles by having the other character roll to break the silence.

If both players are satisfied with the story, they can end the scene by mirroring their introduction. Instead of introducing their own characters, they will summarize each other's characters with a different formula. Start again with the character's name and the way the world sees her and end it with how her character views him.

Hero's Best Friend

Some adventurers travel with trained animals that work as partners in their quests. A hero with an animal companion relies on it for some tasks but understands there are limits to a beast's capabilities.

✸ **To create your animal companion, choose its qualities in the following categories, making sure it has an A, a B, a C, a D, and an E.**

INTELLECT

- O **A.** It seems to have supernatural intelligence. You would not be surprised if it turned out to be a great wizard in an animal form.
- O **B.** You trust the wisdom of this creature more than you trust most people. It knows what to do in most situations without instruction and sometimes despite bad instruction.
- O **C.** This is a capable and quick-learning beast. There are few commands that would not be mastered.
- O **D.** It is able to master the most rudimentary commands, but any idea too advanced gets lost easily.
- O **E.** You do not keep this creature for its powerful mind. Its foolishness often causes both of you a great deal of trouble.

STRENGTH

- O **A.** In battle this beast has no equal. It fights with dauntless fury, striking fear into the hearts of anyone who bears witness to its wrath. On top of strength, it has instinctual skill in combat.
- O **B.** This beast is more powerful than most men will ever be. It is a capable participant in any fight, and you respect it as a combatant more than most allies.
- O **C.** Like any creature, this beast can be dangerous if it needs to be. It is outclassed by skilled fighters and great monsters, but it is more than capable of defending itself.
- O **D.** While this creature probably *can* fight, you have never witnessed it. You'd prefer to keep it out of harm's way when possible. It is more of a liability in battle than an asset.
- O **E.** This creature is a notably frail coward. Its participation in a fight would probably put you and your allies at greater risk.

continued

STEALTH

- O **A.** It moves like a shadow on the wind. It seems to avoid detection with supernatural ease at will. After years of working with this beast, even you are unable to detect it when it does not want to be found.
- O **B.** All but the keenest eyes and sharpest ears are powerless to detect this creature at work. It can find a way into almost any setting completely unnoticed.
- O **C.** It is possible for this creature to be stealthy, but it does not have much training beyond the natural advantages it has as an animal.
- O **D.** This creature is far from graceful or subtle. It would take a wild circumstance to make it an asset in any sort of clandestine activity.
- O **E.** Perhaps due to its shape, size, or color, this creature sticks out in almost every circumstance. Worse yet, it is easily identified as *yours*.

SENSES

- O **A.** You think this creature may possess some kind of supernatural gift for detection. It seems to anticipate events before they begin to unfold. It is capable of finding valuable information without great effort. To call it impressive would be an understatement.
- O **B.** Even for creatures of its type, this beast has impressive senses far beyond those of any humanoid.
- O **C.** Like most animals some of its senses are sharper than a human's, but others are considerably weaker. It is good for specific circumstances.
- O **D.** It may have one strong sense that allows it to function, but you wouldn't dream of setting it to a task like tracking or watch.
- O **E.** Perhaps due to age or injury, this creature lacks key senses. It is only barely functional under the best conditions. You must act as its eyes and ears at all times. It relies on you.

continued

LOYALTY

- **A.** The bond between you and this creature is unbreakable. It would endure any trial to remain at your side. This creature will protect you and the things you care about with dauntless determination.
- **B.** There are few beings living or dead that you would rely on more than this creature. It sees you as family, with an intensity deeper than anything possible in the natural world. Its loyalty is only limited by its capability.
- **C.** You have a close bond with this creature, but it is limited by instinct. There are some circumstances in which animalistic self-preservation outweighs training. Still, in most circumstances it can be relied upon.
- **D.** You have a working relationship with this creature, but there are some areas in which you have distinct trouble. It heeds you because it knows you offer food and stability, but it can be swayed by opportunistic instinct.
- **E.** Calling this creature actively treacherous is probably going too far. Probably. You are still able to work with it, but it has constant behavioral problems, and you get the impression that if you let your guard down, it could turn on you.

56 Unheard Confession

It's fun to have a secret for your character, but it can be difficult to incorporate gracefully. Revealing the secret to other players can be anticlimactic. Keeping something too secret might prevent other players from asking questions. This exercise will create five ways you consciously and unconsciously communicate that you've got a secret.

Appearance

A physical mark on your body is related to your secret. This should be something in a discoverable place that is not immediately obvious. Mentioning it as something seen rarely communicates that it is significant. It should be something you mention every few sessions or so.

EXAMPLES

- A scar in a place that is normally covered by clothing
- A tattoo in a place that is normally covered by clothing
- A braid in your hair normally hidden by the way you tie it
- A symbol etched into your weapon that is visible when you clean/maintain it
- Something embroidered into your cloak over your heart

 ---

Voice

The way you speak is somehow related to a secret you carry. This can be an overt aspect of your character that comes up often but only stands out as odd when measured against the other details of your life.

EXAMPLES

- An accent or dialect
- The use of a particular uncommon name for a common thing
- An uncommon language you speak and occasionally borrow from
- A song you sing to yourself unconsciously when doing menial work
- A word or name that you refuse to say

 ---

continued

Skill

An ability that reflects specialized and uncommon knowledge. You have experience with it due to the secret in your backstory. This should be something you use very rarely, and you are always reluctant to use it.

EXAMPLES

- You carry out an attack not possible for other character classes in your game.
- You recognize enemy techniques in tense situations and provide key insider knowledge.
- You have intimate knowledge of specific esoteric rituals and magical practices.
- You are trained in compensating for a disability you appear not to have.
- You have a reputation or nickname that is not easily explained.

 ....

Action

You have a tic or tell that is almost always present when you are lying. This does not have to be related your secret, but it manifests when you try to cover it up.

EXAMPLES

- A twitch in your eye
- Playing with your hair or ear
- A deadly monotone that suggests agitation
- A habit of changing explanations
- An eccentric ceremony for swearing the truth

 ....

Interaction

You process guilt and the weight of secrecy through behaviors that help you justify it. You have a decipherable code of honor when you interact with others, which can be extrapolated to the context of a larger secret.

EXAMPLES

- You accompany each lie you tell with what you claim is an equivalent truth.
- You do what you consider good deeds to counteract bad ones.
- You excuse yourself without explanation from situations that remind you of your secret.
- You discuss things that happened to you as stories that happened to someone else.
- You ask others about their personal histories often.

 --

A Taste of Death

Adventurers sometimes die and return to life. Explore that experience by answering these prompts.

- **Does your hero treat life differently now that she has died? If so, how?**

- **What was she expecting in an afterlife?**

- **Was that different from what she found?**

- **Has your character discussed her experience with a companion? If not, why does she hide it?**

- **What does your character fear most after this experience?**

- **What is the greatest lesson she carried back from death?**

- **Given the opportunity, would she want to return to life again?**

- **Under what circumstances would your character want to remain dead?**

Conquered Fear

You had five fears before you started adventuring. What moments helped you conquer these fears?

The Body

Fears based around the body are immediate and obvious. They are also almost always reasonable. Being worried about potential harm can keep you alive. A fear of pain or death can also be related to fear of the unknown. That means moving past a fear for your body is not always a positive experience.

REASONS TO TRANSFORM BODILY FEAR

- **Experience:** A fear that becomes reality has the potential to change perspective. One might discover that a scorpion's venom is not as terrifying after surviving a scorpion sting.
- **Perspective:** Learning there are fates more terrifying than your imagination originally envisioned is harrowing, but it can also put lesser concerns to rest.
- **Acceptance:** Some fears can be banished with acceptance. This can be a healthy move to understand mortality or a grim urge to confront morbidity.

 **What event transformed your fear?**

The Mind

Mental fears are often puzzles that need to be unraveled. Most fears are built out of simple biological concerns. In the mind they can be ill defined and complex—difficult to express, let alone conquer. Many fears based in the mental space are smaller concerns that have metamorphosed into behemoths far in excess of their component parts.

continued

APPROACHES TO TRANSFORMING MENTAL FEAR

- **Introspection:** Understanding yourself is the key to untangling nameless fears that haunt the mind. Many adventurers are focused on the mission ahead, but taking the time to address personal concerns can prepare you to face your tasks with clarity.
- **Aid:** Few people ever do anything alone. A hero who opens her- or himself to others risks pain but gains allies who can care for her or him. Some problems are best approached from the outside.
- **Therapy:** It may be a simple matter of taking the time to care for a concern and soothe it. Adventurers mostly solve their problems by drawing a sword and charging into action, but some beasts can only be slain with time and care.

 **When you look back on your mental fear, what do you think of it?**

The Soul

Even in a world where good and evil are forces that can be detected and measured, the realm of the soul is governed by faith. The existential threat of evil is tied to someone's personal beliefs. The thing that separates those who cower in the face of darkness from those who stand against it is the belief that the darkness can be conquered.

ROOTS OF BELIEF

- **Belief in self:** Believing that you cannot be corrupted and that you have the power to stand against those who have been is all you need to dismiss most spiritual fear.
- **Belief in others:** Holding the conviction that certain people or social qualities are worthy opponents to darkness is a powerful shield against spiritual fear. You don't need to believe that you personally can banish evil in order to stand against it if you trust that you are not alone.

- **Belief in a higher power:** Having faith that there are forces as powerful and mysterious as the horrors you face is enough to give you the courage to confront the unimaginable.

What do you think of when confronted with harrowing darkness?

The Heart

The heart is tied up in other people. Fears of the heart are built around social anxiety. Ironically, the remedy for these fears also rests in social structures. Fear of being rejected by one group is easily banished when you find acceptance with another. Social concerns can be easily drowned out by social comforts.

SOCIAL STRONGHOLDS

- **A partner:** A partner is someone you can trust entirely, whose opinion matters to you. It is easy to ignore stress from other places if you can rely on one person to help sort through the chaos.
- **A family:** Families are more chaotic than partners. They can be the source of great social stress, but they have an underlying permanence that offers stability.
- **Friends:** A group of people defined by their mutual enjoyment of one another's company is crucial to escape interpersonal horror. Friends offer escape and therapeutic reprieve.

Whom do you confide in when the world seems to be set against you?

The Beast

The beast has many forms. It slides into every realm of fear, enhancing and underscoring what is already there. There are two ways of dealing with the beast, and they are both, sadly, temporary remedies:

- **Confirming absence:** Many claim that knowledge conquers fear. To an extent this is true. The beast fills in gaps in your knowledge, deepening shadows in your mind. When you learn about the true nature of things, you banish traces of the beast from your thoughts.
- **Obscuring presence:** On rare occasions more accurate knowledge of the world can actually unleash the beast. Discovering a problem is larger and more immediately dangerous than you first realized courts the beast. Focusing on a complicated web of issues you can't solve locks you in fear. In order to function, sometimes you have to narrow your focus so you are not conquered by the enormity of your task. A distraction that allows you to even momentarily leave the beast's shadow can also provide fortitude.

What circumstance brought you to confront the beast?

What do you tell yourself about this experience in order to keep yourself functional?

Getting to Know You

We learn a lot about our companions by traveling with them. However, some information needs to be uncovered intentionally. This game invites you to pick the party member you know the least about and challenges you to learn ten things about him or her. To add a challenge, you have to roll to determine which method you will have to use to find your answer.

What will you discover? (roll a d10)

1. What qualities make this character respect a person?
2. Whom does she trust most?
3. Where would he rather be?
4. Who raised them?
5. What secret does he wish to uncover?
6. Whom does she consider an enemy?
7. Have they ever fallen in love?
8. What is her most strongly held belief?
9. What does he think of children?
10. Does she consider you a worthy companion?

How will you discover it? (roll a d6)

1. Directly asking him
2. Sharing information about yourself to get some in return
3. Enlisting an agent to find the answer for you
4. Finding an answer based on careful study
5. Using magic or divine divination
6. Using deceit or trickery

A Show of Force

Not every challenge an adventurer faces is a worthy test of strength. Some legends are born when a hero takes on a challenge well beneath his, her, or their skill. In this scenario an arrogant and intoxicated fool targets you with harassment.

✸ **Decide how you would react, making sure to end the scenario with at least one A, B, C, D, and E.**

Your party settles in to enjoy food and drinks at a local tavern. There is music and merriment all around, but one particularly intoxicated individual has been eyeing you with disgust. His glaring gradually changes to unpleasant comments and off-color jokes. His companions seem amused, and that emboldens him to project his performance to anyone who will listen. His mocking voice all but challenges you directly. The longer you ignore him, the more cruel he becomes.

- O **A.** You pointedly ignore this ridiculous display until he says something completely unforgivable. You calmly set down your drink, and the light in the room seems to dim with your mood. The chatter in the bar quiets until the focus is on you.
- O **B.** You had not noticed the drunk for a good portion of his ranting, which was fortunate for him. However, the clear discomfort of your companions has drawn your attention to the situation. You roll your eyes and glare at the fool who has disrupted your evening.
- O **C.** You have been taught when to fight and when to hold back. This man is clearly beneath your attention. You stand up and calmly try to de-escalate the situation.
- O **D.** You noticed this pathetic creature's cruelty the moment he opened his mouth and you've been quietly seething. You stand.
- O **E.** Despite calls from your companions to remain calm, you pick up your drink and hurl it across the room, causing the glass to shatter dangerously close to the man's head.

Not able or willing to pick up on the gravity of the situation, the drunk smiles wickedly and approaches you with a swagger.

- **A.** He moves toward you with what he probably imagines is a predatory grin on his face as the wiser folks he was talking to shrink away from him. He does not realize that he now faces you alone.
- **B.** He slurs another insult toward you, but even his supporters seem confused about his meaning. You respond with a particularly witty metaphor about his appearance and personality. A good portion of the tavern appears to appreciate this. He does not.
- **C.** He takes a sloppy swing at you. With a graceful step, you are easily out of harm's way. This seems to make him angrier.
- **D.** Before he can speak again, you launch an attack that strikes him firmly in the nose. He looks to you in shock, blood on his face, tears in his eyes.
- **E.** He stops just in front of you and grabs one of your companions' drink. He pulls it to his lips and makes a show of sipping it before he pours what remains over your head. The tavern is so silent you can hear the individual drops of the liquid as they fall to the floor.

He lunges forward, bigotry no longer capable of being expressed in words. He is now a snarling beast moved by petty hatred.

- **A.** You respond with liquid grace, stepping into and past the attack, causing him to injure himself with his clumsy assault. Some tavern goers hold back snickering as he reels from his own stupidity. You speak in a calm, measured tone that silences the amused parties surrounding you.
- **B.** With several movements too fast for the eye to follow, you strike him before he can touch you, sending him reeling back into a dense support beam. There is an audible thud as his head connects with the unforgiving wood.

- C. He grabs hold of you by your shoulders, but you grab back. A force stronger than he could have imagined throws him into the air and onto his back. Those who do not know you by name or reputation stare at you, mouths agape.
- D. His fist connects with you, but you remain unmoved. His eyes meet yours, and you detect the disbelief of a man who knows he is about to lose. With a bright and wicked smile, you send him hurtling back into his table, causing it to collapse under him.
- E. You take a few hits while his friends cheer him on. They do not know that you did this so you could gauge his strength. They will know very soon.

Snarling with a desperation fueled by rage, alcohol, and adrenaline, he reaches to his belt and draws a dagger. The blade gleams wickedly in the dim light of the tavern. It is clear that this has alarmed some of the others in his party, but he is beyond their influence. The oaf lumbers toward you once more with murder in his eyes.

- A. To an untrained observer, it appears as though he slumps to the ground of his own accord. Experienced adventurers know better. You struck at him with the power they have been bracing for since this altercation started. Faster than sight and without apparent effort, you subdue the fool. A few of the more cynical heroes of experience mutter that he is lucky to be alive.
- B. You strike decisively with perhaps more force and flair than were strictly necessary. The room is illuminated by the dazzling sight of you. Even those who could not understand exactly who you were at the beginning of this altercation get a sense of what you are capable of.
- C. You pound your fist onto an adjacent table, sending a heavy iron plate into the air and your waiting hand. You easily parry his clumsy stabs before striking him firmly on the nose with the edge of your tableware. There is a soft crack as his nose breaks. The dagger falls from his hands as he raises them to his face, wailing in agony.

- O **D.** Momentarily surprised, you stumble to gain advantage in the melee. Your companions almost rush to your aid before you let out a battle cry, sending an attack toward your assailant just as his dagger nicks you in a nonvital area. You are wounded, but your blow is decisive. Your opponent crumples to the ground in a heap.
- O **E.** You dodge his clumsy slashes, careful to keep him from injuring onlookers with his wild swings. Slash after slash finds nothing but air as you lead him in tight circles. His rage-filled cries turn to labored gasps as sweat beads on his brow. The blows lose their strength as fatigue overtakes him. When the moment is right, you carefully take control of his arm and force the blade back into its sheath. He wheezes as the rest of the tavern stares at you in awe. The moment is spoiled as he vomits on your boots.

There is a beat of relieved silence as onlookers realize the battle is over.

- O **A.** The tavern lights up with cheers and applause. Your table is sent drinks by adventurers who admire your skill. By the end of the evening, the bar is a chorus of enthusiastically off-key covers of the song some clever bard improvised based on the story. You will remember this night fondly.
- O **B.** A rasping laugh from a venerable fighter cuts through the silence. Your attacker's friends sheepishly gather him up and take him outside to recover. Not everyone in your party approves of how you handled the situation. The rest of the evening is filled with wild hypotheticals, boasting, and the recounting of similar stories of petty triumph. You go to bed satisfied.

- O **C.** Someone takes advantage of the silence to order a new drink. Within seconds the sound of activity and conversation returns the tavern to business as usual. You resume your seat, feeling the obvious approval and disapproval of your comrades before you continue your night as though nothing had happened.
- O **D.** The silence is quickly brought to an end as you hear a crash from across the room. It seems some other sod took advantage of the display to settle a score of his own. People are quick to intervene this time, but their actions are either too late or inadequate. Soon the majority of the tavern is engulfed in a raucous brawl. It is not long before the melee reaches you and your companions. Soon you are fighting back-to-back with reckless abandon.
- O **E.** The angry bark of the bartender cuts through the air. It seems he doesn't care who started the fight; he just wants everyone involved to get out. While you could probably push back, it hardly seems worth the effort. You and your companions pay and exit to a cool night. You spend the rest of the evening with your party, walking through the town, cooling down from the excitement.

Five Times Your Name Was Cursed

Adventurers tend to upset people. Not being bound by conventional laws and disrupting the status quo everywhere you travel will do that. The best adventurers have heard many people shout angry expletives at their backs.

 **Answer the prompts and select details to create dramatic scenes from your adventuring past.**

A Bystander

During one of your escapades, you damaged a piece of private property. You were too busy to care at the time, but the owner either saw it happen or was shocked to find it. Describe what you broke and how it happened:

How did you respond to the event? (choose one)

- O I didn't even think about it.
- O I apologized in the moment, and that's enough.
- O I eventually sent compensation to the owner.
- O I repaired the damage myself.

A Rival

In the course of a contentious professional relationship, you dazzled a rival with a moment of brilliant competence and ingenuity. Her knowledge of you and the field in which you compete was enough to let her know how impressive you are. Describe your moment of victory:

How did your rival respond? (choose one)

- O By learning from you
- O By working to match you
- O By creating an underhanded advantage
- O By giving up in frustration

An Authority

Your action severely disrupted an orderly tradition, ceremony, or event to the point it has permanently changed. Years later, a new status quo exists despite the reservations of the powers that be. What moment of boldness inspired a change?

What did that moment spark? (choose one)

- O Wonder
- O Self-expression
- O Revolution
- O Dissolution

An Enemy

You disrupted the plans of a superior foe. Without your interference he stood to reap a substantial gain since he had accounted for everything but you. Describe the moment your enemy discovered his plan had failed:

✵ What does he feel when he thinks of it now? (choose one)

- O Rage
- O Annoyance
- O Humiliation
- O Reluctant respect

Yourself

You have made many mistakes over the course of your life. One is central to your sense of self. It is something that created or underscored a truth about you that you find unpleasant. What happened as a result of this mistake?

✵ How did you grow from this? (choose one)

- O I accepted a limit.
- O I committed to change.
- O I looked for help.
- O I became disillusioned.

Mountains and Molehills

In improvisational theater performers are taught to make their scene partners look important. This means reacting to other performers' decisions by making them important to your character. On stage this makes scenes more dramatic and helps establish character relationships. This same principle holds true at the gaming table. This exercise will help you make a possibly innocuous statement into an opportunity for interesting role-play.

Pick something a PC said to your character in the last session.
It should be something he or she said to you directly. It doesn't have to be about you; it just has to be clear the PC was talking to you when he or she said it.

Write or paraphrase it here:

How did this make your character feel?
This doesn't have to be rational. People react unreasonably to innocuous statements all the time. Grounding your reaction in an emotion makes it easy to take it to interesting places and means whatever you are feeling will ultimately be resolved through role-play.

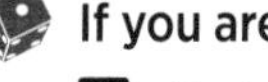

If you are having trouble thinking of an emotion, roll a d6:

1. Embarrassed
2. Defensive
3. Afraid
4. Joyous
5. Prideful
6. Grateful

How could this emotion have been provoked?
Emotional reactions don't need to be grounded or justified. A character might not understand why she feels a certain way; all she knows is that she does. As the player, you can decide if a character is misinterpreting something, projecting a separate feeling into a new area, or genuinely processing something one of her companions said to her.

Take your idea to the other player so you can collaborate on your story.
This ensures you are both happy to explore the story, which means you'll be able to work together to make each moment satisfying. Your GM controls fate and circumstance, and can work to put your characters into situations where things they are feeling are forced to the surface. Even if you don't need the GM's involvement, letting her or him know you are pursuing this sort of story is a good idea. Characters outside the two involved in the conflict can provide counsel, meddle to try and fix things, or bask in the chaos of emotional turmoil.

Explore what the emotion means to your character privately.
Decide how your character works through periods of heightened emotion. Is he aware of what he is feeling? If so, does he know why?

Possible responses:

- Writing in a journal
- Prayer and meditation
- Physical training
- Playing music
- Working on a craft
- Cleaning or organizing
- Drinking
- Hunting
- Shopping

Indirectly express that emotion publicly.
Issues based on miscommunication are made worse when people don't talk about them. That's bad for relationships in real life but great for relationships in stories. It's more satisfying to watch characters finally hash something out after they have spent time dancing around the issue. To build up to a satisfying conclusion, hint at the issue through indirect behavior.

If you are having trouble deciding how to communicate indirectly, try one of these approaches:

- Make excuses to be close to the other character.
- Laugh at unexpected moments.
- Create opportunities for the other character to make similar statements.
- Make mistakes doing tasks your character is good at.
- Have your character change something about his or her appearance.
- Have your character approach eating or drinking differently.
- Speak differently toward everyone in the party.
- Give the other character preferential or differential treatment.
- Break something.

Confront the Situation

Work with the other player and your GM to put the characters in a situation where they are forced to speak directly. The goal is to address the situation and resolve it by the characters revealing something new about themselves. Ending a story like this with a discovery is important because it means something happened. In real life you can be taken on an emotional roller-coaster for no reason. In stories we have the opportunity to make every interaction significant. If you want a shift in character dynamics, the new discovery and emotional drama can be catalysts for that change. If you'd prefer to maintain the status quo, that discovery can underscore why the established dynamic works.

Life Goes On

Adventurers can leave a lot of chaos in their wake. It is rare that a party has time to stop and clean up its own messes. Even so, the world continues to turn after monumental battles and heroic feats. For this exercise take the scene of one of your hardest-fought battles. Follow the scene through time to see what that place becomes.

Describe a place that you and your party have left behind. This can be an in-depth image or bullet points of different details that stand out in your mind. Having a clear sense of place is important because it will give you a good foundation for the exercise. You could start anywhere:

- The tavern where you first met
- The room where you all first confronted the primary villain of your campaign
- The field where your camp was ambushed by monsters
- The inn you stayed at a few towns back
- The home you left behind

 **Roll a d6 to determine the force that causes change:**

1. **Weather:** The area is changed by the power of the earth: wind, rain, fire, lighting, or any nonliving natural force. There are signs of flood, ashy waste, sun-bleached bones, frozen tundra, or bog-preserved corpses.
2. **Life:** Changes are made by nonintelligent living things such as plants and animals. You see moss, flowers, bodies picked over by scavenging beasts, and new life.
3. **Individuals:** The area has been changed by intelligent creatures working alone. Memorials, graffiti, and small efforts to clean and rebuild are all present.
4. **Industry:** Changes have been made by large groups of organized, intelligent creatures working toward a common goal. There are new developments paving over what once stood and large monuments.
5. **Magic:** Changes were brought about by supernatural or divine forces without individual intervention. Miracles, hauntings, and magic phenomena abound.
6. **Entropy:** Change has been made by erosion, rot, and death. The absence of growth and the destruction of what remains are the most striking features of the area.

Now, depending on what agency of change you picked, describe the main changes after each of these periods.

1 Week

----

continued

1 Month

1 Year

10 Years

100 Years

In the Eye of My Enemy

When someone who knows you well is looking for you, what specific markers does she seek to follow your trail?

- **How does she describe you to strangers?** An enemy who knows you well is able to distill your description down to a few iconic elements. What about you is unforgettable?

- **What does she look for on a battlefield?** When searching a battlefield for signs of your involvement, how does she know which slashes and spells are yours? It could be the strength or finesse evident in the wounds on fallen foes or the destructive force behind your magic. What makes her grimly utter, "He was here"?

- **What does she tell her minions?** When sending servants to attack you, what does your enemy say makes you dangerous?

- **How does she lure you?** If an enemy who truly understood your motives were to construct a trap, what would she use as bait?

- **How does she underestimate you?** What assumption would a foe who knows you intimately make? Why would it be wrong?

Irrational Taste

Preparing for long journeys is a necessity for most adventurers. Acquiring peculiar tastes is both an unintended side effect and a survival strategy. Not many will steal your rations if they would never consider touching them in the first place. Here are some suggestions on what to pack.

1. Something Hard to Chew

It can be dried, smoked, salted, or otherwise dehydrated, but it has more in common with leather than it does with other foods.

What is it made of?

How does it smell?

---

2. A Powerful Spice

In desperate situations you need something strong to hide hints of rot.

What does it taste like?

How must you store it?

---

3. Something to Keep You Awake

Being able to focus on lonely watch shifts is a valuable skill. Having something to keep you alert is one of the best ways to ensure you (and the rest of your party) will make it to the next watch.

How do you use it?

Is it easy to find?

---

4. Something to Keep Your Attention

It can be a book, map, craft, or puzzle, anything to keep your focus when there is nothing else to do.

How long have you had it?

Do you believe you have mastered it?

Fish Story

Acts of heroism have a certain...flexibility. Yes, they happened, but in the retelling of tales, details tend to shift. The same story can be wildly different based on who is in the audience.

Pick one of your past adventures. Roll a d6 to discover how you exaggerate the story for the various audiences.

1. **Raising Stakes:** Your reasons for performing your heroic deed become progressively nobler. An injured companion becomes a group of sickly orphans.
2. **Underdog:** Your resources and general health diminish to the point of absurdity. A simple duel becomes a fight in which you had no weapons or armor while holding a wound closed.
3. **Dramatic Backdrop:** The world around you shifts to match the mood of the moment in your tale. Sunny days become brutal storms; a cave turns into an active volcano.
4. **Vast Rewards:** Any treasure or wealth multiplies in age, value, and quantity. A purse of gold becomes a dragon's hoard.
5. **Fearsome Foes:** Any opponents grow in size, number, and cruelty. A band of highwaymen turns into an army of man-eating trolls.
6. **Courageous Action:** Actions by you and your companions become inspired moments of breathtaking genius and miraculous coincidence. A simple sword stroke becomes a perfectly calculated fatal strike.

Now that you know how the story is changing, picture who you might be telling it to. What follows are potential audiences for your tale. Under each audience write down what changes about your story depending on whom you tell it to. In a few sentences, explain one of your past adventures.

continued

Fellow adventurers at a tavern...

A bard composing a song...

A potential lover...

A wide-eyed child...

A judge ruling on your case...

You Have No Idea

You task your familiar with a simple job, which it completes diligently despite nightmarish complications. Roll dice to create foundational story details and answer prompts to see where they take you.

 **Roll a d6 to give your familiar a seemingly easy task:**

1. To collect a crucial ingredient
2. To watch something vulnerable
3. To find information
4. To keep a situation orderly
5. To tidy a mess
6. To stay out of the way and not cause problems

This is important because: (choose two)

- It involves something you both care for.
- Lives are on the line.
- You are both trying to impress someone.
- Time is of the essence.
- The familiar recently failed a task and wants to make up for it.

THERE ARE COMPLICATIONS...

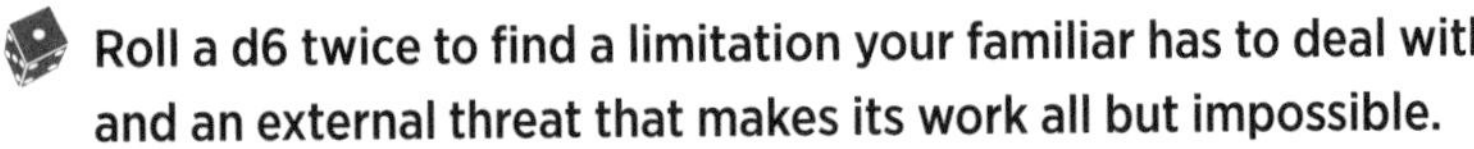

Roll a d6 twice to find a limitation your familiar has to deal with and an external threat that makes its work all but impossible.

continued

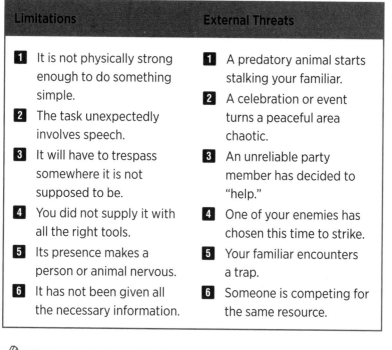

Limitations	External Threats
1 It is not physically strong enough to do something simple.	1 A predatory animal starts stalking your familiar.
2 The task unexpectedly involves speech.	2 A celebration or event turns a peaceful area chaotic.
3 It will have to trespass somewhere it is not supposed to be.	3 An unreliable party member has decided to "help."
4 You did not supply it with all the right tools.	4 One of your enemies has chosen this time to strike.
5 Its presence makes a person or animal nervous.	5 Your familiar encounters a trap.
6 It has not been given all the necessary information.	6 Someone is competing for the same resource.

What gets destroyed in the process of completing this task?

What indignity does your familiar suffer?

How does your familiar set things right before you return?

What small problem do you notice when your familiar miraculously presents you with the fruits of its labor?

The Gauntlet

Heroes are usually remembered for their accomplishments, but there is a great deal of punishment that leads to those moments of triumph.

Following is a checklist of wild wounds and injuries. Check off ones that your character experiences on her or his path to glory. How far can she or he go before retiring?

- O Stabbed by a dagger
- O Cut by a sword
- O Pierced by a spear
- O Crushed by a mace
- O Smashed by a hammer
- O Sliced by an axe
- O Slashed by a polearm
- O Lashed by a whip
- O Struck by arrows
- O Burned by fire
- O Burned by magic
- O Shocked by magic
- O Frozen by magic
- O Battered with force
- O Drained by negative energy
- O Scorched by radiant energy
- O Burned by acid
- O Psychically punctured
- O Sonically smacked
- O Balefully transfigured
- O Broken by otherworldly madness

- Disintegrated
- Touched annihilation magic
- Tasted poison
- Fell into a pit
- Pierced by a trap
- Slashed by a trap
- Bludgeoned by a trap
- Magically harmed by a trap
- Fell from a cliff
- Bitten
- Pecked
- Mauled by claws
- Raked with talons
- Thrashed with tentacles
- Swarmed
- Enveloped by an ooze
- Stepped on
- Swallowed whole
- Fooled by an illusion
- Charmed by enchantment
- Teleported into danger
- Merged with a physical object
- Turned to goo
- Grappled
- Blinded
- Deafened
- Exhausted
- Fatigued
- Frightened
- Grappled
- Incapacitated
- Paralyzed
- Drowned
- Dismembered
- Disfigured
- Turned to stone
- Knocked prone
- Restrained (nonconsensually)
- Stunned
- Rendered unconscious
- Killed
- Resurrected
- Reincarnated
- Made undead
- Soul removed, placed in gem
- Unwritten from time
- Wished to oblivion

Honey Pot

Adventurers must often contend with clever foes. Devious creatures lay traps, using the best and worst qualities a hero has against her or him. Spotting something too good to be true or otherwise out of the ordinary can save your life. All that begins with knowing yourself. Answer the prompts to understand what your triggers are.

What opportunity would be too important to walk away from?

What vice do you jump at the chance to indulge?

What call to action could you never bring yourself to ignore?

What fear has the power to overwhelm your reason?

Who would you give almost anything to see?

Whom or what have you sworn to destroy?

70 Trusty Steed

As a committed adventurer, you need a hero's mount—one with speed, courage, strength, mobility, and endurance.

✸ **Select the qualities of your steed, ensuring they have at least one A, B, C, D, and E.**

SPEED

- O **A.** Your mount is the fastest creature of its kind. It is capable of routinely pulling off feats described as impossible. If time is of the essence, this beast is up to the task.
- O **B.** Your mount has only been bested in a contest of speed once or twice. When other adventurers discuss the fastest beasts in the land, yours is always mentioned.
- O **C.** Your beast is dependably swift. While it is no racing mount, you have always made good time on its back. It has the normal limitations of creatures of its type.
- O **D.** Although this creature is reliable in other ways, it will win no prize for speed. It always lags behind other beasts.
- O **E.** This creature is reliable but slow. Your journeys always take longer than you think they will.

COURAGE

- O **A.** Your beast is undaunted in the face of apocalyptic cataclysm. Even if it is not intelligent enough to grasp the importance of your work, it pursues your mission with unwavering focus. Sometimes its courage outstrips your own.
- O **B.** In the heat of battle, this beast is fearless. It can only be turned by events that would break most humanoids.
- O **C.** This creature is reliable in battle and storm, but there are some situations that reduce it to its base instincts.
- O **D.** While this beast can be relied upon for hauling and long trips, at the first sign of battle, it will spook and possibly cause damage.
- O **E.** This creature is a natural-born coward. It will run or hide at the first sign of trouble and a few signs that aren't.

STRENGTH

- **A.** With the proper harness, this creature could move mountains. It can do the work of an army of draft horses, all without complaint or ceremony.
- **B.** This creature is worth more than a dozen creatures of its type, able to move tons of weight without proper rigging. It is the wonder and envy of everyone.
- **C.** Your partner is capable of handling a large amount of weight but not much more than another creature of its type. Over your years together, there have been more than a few challenges well beyond its capability.
- **D.** This is not a creature built for labor. It can handle smaller tasks, but you know you can't charge it with work meant for most creatures of its kind.
- **E.** There is little use for this creature beyond riding and perhaps carrying some small personal effects.

MOBILITY

- **A.** There is no terrain or condition that can turn this beast. It can cut through water, air, and the worst the land has to offer. This creature could reliably ride through an earthquake, an erupting volcano, and a hurricane all at once.
- **B.** Even in inclement conditions, this beast can be trusted to protect you and itself. It is not capable of producing miracles, but there are some who insist that it does.
- **C.** You feel comfortable taking this creature into many difficult situations. However, you are aware it has the normal limitations of other creatures of its type.
- **D.** This creature has an injury or inherent weakness that makes it vulnerable in certain situations. You are careful to watch over it and must think carefully about when you decide to rely on it.
- **E.** It might be age or injury, but there is something that makes this creature vulnerable to inclement conditions. Without perfect conditions, this creature runs the serious risk of injury.

continued

ENDURANCE

- O **A.** This beast can work on until the earth beneath it grinds to oblivion. It will fight through any injury with fierce determination. As long as it has breath to draw and a heart to beat, it will move.
- O **B.** This creature can work longer than most would even be able to watch. With little rest, food, or water, it can do the work of many creatures of its type.
- O **C.** This beast is admirable, but it has the limitations of most mortal beings. Without proper care, it will tire.
- O **D.** While it is dependable once or twice a day, any sustained effort will make this creature tire.
- O **E.** Due to age, injury, or perhaps laziness, this beast is all but useless. It will not move for anyone but you.

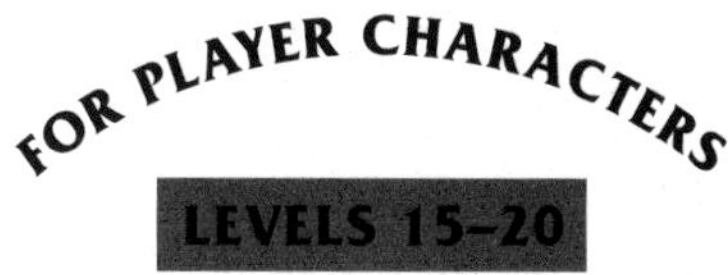

Myths and Legends

71 Towers of Terror

You just moved into your dream neighborhood only to find your most hated rival has purchased a tower right next to yours. Open conflict would destroy the universe, so you settle the score by building a house designed to annoy him.

72 Monuments

One of your character's deeds has permanently shaped his or her world. How does he or she feel looking at it? This helps create a physical element of a setting tied to the reader's character through writing prompts.

73 Classifying Villains

When creating or combating villains, it's important to know how to classify them. Understanding aspects of their personalities, behavior, and aesthetics might tell you more than their alignment.

74 Home Heraldry

Create your own coat of arms to reflect who you and your family are.

75 "It Is My Distinct Pleasure to Announce..."

You were invited to a royal gala. The page sent over to confirm your attendance bashfully informs you that the name you have provided is not sufficient, and he requires greater detail.

76 God, No

In recognition of your great deeds, a prominent deity has announced he or she will attend a feast you are throwing. It may be the god in question, the plans you had for your feast, or the company you already invited, but you know this is going to be a disaster.

77 Five Commandments

There are five rules observed by creatures in your service. They are the first lessons you teach and the foundation of any world shaped in your image.

78 Pocket Dimension

The weird, wonderful place to which you escape in order to be yourself. How does it reflect your interests?

79 For the Myth That Has Everything

Your allies have the power to split mountains, part seas, and walk between raindrops. What gift could be worthy of them?

80 Inventory

Create a list of things your character refuses to throw away.

81 Art of Facts

Legends of your deeds have spread far and wide. Accompanying those tales are stories about the items you carry, which are myths in their own right.

82 Terror of Wisdom

There are five things mortals do not fear. Your experience has taught you to fear them. A lot.

83 A Cutlass Carol

Three ghosts visit you to show you visions of the past, present, and future in hope of teaching you a lesson. The problem is the lesson isn't really worth learning.

84 Private Secrets

Create a mystery your character has left in his or her wake, one that adventurers and scholars will be pondering for years to come.

85 It Sounds Good on Paper

Create artifacts that hold caveats making them significantly less attractive in practice.

86 I Knew Them Well

Pick a mythic figure or deity in the setting and detail information your character knows about him or her (or it).

87 Alive Only in Memory

You know of a place that no longer exists.

88 Collecting Dust

In your home you have objects on your mantel that many believe are lost to time and that some would be shocked to learn exist at all. What are these things, and how do you treat them?

89 Sign of a Legend

There is a symbol or mark that has become associated with your name. This exercise tells you what it is, where it appears, and the truths/falsehoods that circulate about it.

90 Hobby

In addition to the skills you picked up as a heroic adventurer, you also mastered a mundane craft and honed it to legendary perfection. This will tell you what that is and what impact it had on yourself and the world.

91 Five Lives

Your deeds have touched five individuals. Who are they, and what became of them?

92 You Made It Weird

The chimera, the owlbear, the gibbering mouther: beloved monsters created by powerful beings as a bizarre form of competition. This exercise will help you take an existing monster and make it into something truly strange.

93 In the Eyes of Mortals

What do different people see when they look at you? You will see yourself through the eyes of a watchman, a bartender, a pickpocket, a king, and a child.

94 Hangover

At some point last night, you lost a powerful artifact. Now if you could just remember last night. Retrace your steps to reclaim what is yours.

95 Apprentice

A priority-based aspect creator that works like the mentor game: talent, ego, reliability, studiousness, morality.

96 Five Enemies

A look at some of the foes you have faced in your past.

97

Impossible Trial

You are inundated with requests from potential students clearly unworthy of your knowledge. What tasks do you set for them, expecting them to fail?

98

Not Looking to Get Merlined

When do you decide that your apprentice doesn't have your best interests at heart?

99

Crisis of Faith

Faith works differently in a world where gods routinely grant miraculous power, speak to their followers, and occasionally appear in the mortal realm. Believers do not question their existence, only their intentions.

100

Your Kind of King

Your life of adventuring has ended with you sitting on the throne. A hero becoming a ruler is always a unique story. Fill in this chart to see what kind of ruler you would be.

Towers of Terror

You just moved into your dream neighborhood only to find your most hated rival has purchased a tower right next to yours. Open conflict would destroy the universe, so you settle the score by building a house designed to annoy him. Make choices to participate in a supernatural neighborhood rivalry.

Your distaste for this person knows no bounds. Roll a d6 to discover that it stems from:

1. A lifelong rivalry
2. A comment you thought you overheard at a party
3. The cosmic game of chess you play against each other through surrogates and servants
4. His ostentatious and self-important manner of dress
5. A flippantly critical review of your autobiographical epic poem
6. You actually can't remember, but this rivalry has been going on too long to stop now

He is a... (roll a d6 or write in your own idea)

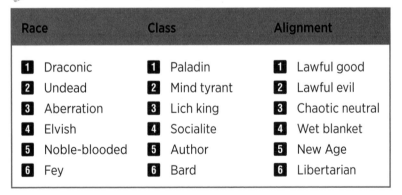

Race	Class	Alignment
1 Draconic	1 Paladin	1 Lawful good
2 Undead	2 Mind tyrant	2 Lawful evil
3 Aberration	3 Lich king	3 Chaotic neutral
4 Elvish	4 Socialite	4 Wet blanket
5 Noble-blooded	5 Author	5 New Age
6 Fey	6 Bard	6 Libertarian

You cannot move your home because...

1. You have a perfect view of the lake
2. You just found a tile that *really* works in the master bathroom
3. This house has been in your family for generations
4. This was land appointed to you by the crown
5. You hear big moves can be stressful for hirelings
6. You won't give him the satisfaction

In order to drive him away, you have to engineer your home to offend his sensibilities. If you can add six offensive elements to your home, you will be successful. However, if your additions exceed twenty points, you'll be blocked by the homeowner's association (HOA) and forced to live near your most hated rival forever.

Roll for random additions with a point cost equal to the roll.

Animals	Noise
1 Install a bird feeder on your road verge	1 Learn the saxophone
2 Become a hobbyist beekeeper	2 Teach tap dancing in your backyard
3 Adopt ten large beagles	3 Open an all-seasons caroling club
4 Begin raising endangered screaming butterflies	4 Breed hydrangeas that sing at sunrise
5 Gift him a white elephant	5 Host weekly fireworks viewings in your backyard
6 Hire a pied piper to attract rats and children to his yard	6 Hold group therapy meetings for at-risk banshees

continued

View	Sabotage
1 Construct a fence on your property to inhibit his view of the lake	**1** Teleport a faulty septic system onto his property
2 Paint the shutters facing his house a ghastly yellow	**2** Enchant the mirrors in his house to reflect him as he truly is
3 Introduce horrific abominations to the lake that cause madness on sight	**3** Pay every cleaning service in the area not to work with him
4 Install a series of glass orb decorations that always reflect light into his windows	**4** Hire dwarfs to engineer a sinkhole on his property
5 Commission a twenty-foot marble nude statue of yourself for your backyard	**5** Open a portal to the shadow realm in his pantry
6 Cast a See Invisible spell on his windows and host swingers' parties for ghosts on your property	**6** Fill his pipes with water elementals who reduce his water pressure

continued

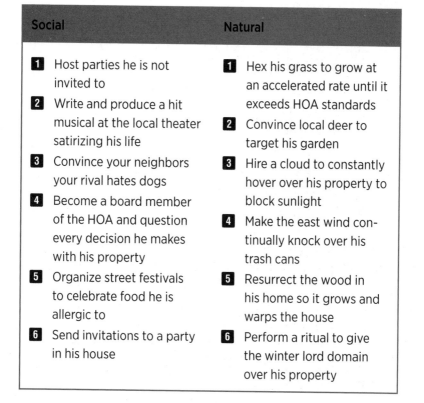

Social	Natural
1 Host parties he is not invited to	**1** Hex his grass to grow at an accelerated rate until it exceeds HOA standards
2 Write and produce a hit musical at the local theater satirizing his life	**2** Convince local deer to target his garden
3 Convince your neighbors your rival hates dogs	**3** Hire a cloud to constantly hover over his property to block sunlight
4 Become a board member of the HOA and question every decision he makes with his property	**4** Make the east wind continually knock over his trash cans
5 Organize street festivals to celebrate food he is allergic to	**5** Resurrect the wood in his home so it grows and warps the house
6 Send invitations to a party in his house	**6** Perform a ritual to give the winter lord domain over his property

72 Monuments

One of your character's deeds has permanently shaped their world. Anyone who gazes upon it understands it as the work of an unfathomably powerful being. Start by choosing some facts about its nature and relationship with the world, then answer the prompts.

Choose two:

- ○ It can be seen from miles away.
- ○ To this day scholars still debate about aspects of it.
- ○ It possesses properties that make it valuable to ordinary people.
- ○ Some groups make pilgrimages to visit it as a holy site.
- ○ It has been incorporated into a larger memorial.
- ○ It fills some people with a sense of dread or fear.
- ○ It will stand for more than a thousand years.
- ○ It is a testament to your great power.
- ○ It is a testament to your undaunted virtue.

What does it look like?

Do people live nearby, and is it someplace that can be easily reached?

What sort of relationship does the average person have with this thing?

Was the day you created it a particularly momentous occasion?

What did you do to change the land in such a way?

Has nature embraced your monument or rejected it?

When you look at this monument, whom or what do you think of?

What do you feel when you think about it?

73 Classifying Villains

When creating or combating villains, it's important to know how to classify them. Understanding aspects of their personality, behavior, and aesthetics might tell you more than their alignment.

✸ **Choose from the following characteristics for your creations or foes to gain insight into their character.**

Danger

Understanding what makes a villain dangerous and how that danger manifests is critical. As a GM, this understanding gives you insight into which situations cause your villains to thrive and lets you know when they perish. As a hero, it lets you know when to be afraid and when to strike.

- O **Mastermind:** A creature that behaves with calculated forethought. On the high end, you have someone who plans wicked deeds with genius precision. On the low end, you have dimwitted or impulsive creatures.
- O **Force of Nature:** Something that behaves instinctually or perhaps even mindlessly.
- O **Strong:** A creature or force that produces deliberate and overt harm. It is easy to understand and difficult to conquer.
- O **Subtle:** A creature that attacks indirectly or has no obvious way to be interacted with. This could be a physically weak creature or a force that is simply inscrutable and understated.

Behavior

Even villains of a similar type react to motivating stimuli differently. Charting this behavior as a GM will dictate how to faithfully react to player choices. Charting it as a hero will help you navigate the risk of striking your most dangerous foes.

continued

- **Vindictive:** The type of creature that holds grudges and refuses to suffer insult. Anything that inflicts curses or plots revenge.
- **Callous:** A villain unconcerned with people or a force that is incapable of empathy.
- **Cruel:** A creature that commits horrible acts because it delights in pain and suffering.
- **Dispassionate:** A creature that commits horrible acts due to its nature or duty. It derives neither joy nor pleasure from evil, but it is committed to it nonetheless.

Aesthetic

Understanding a villain's aesthetic is mostly important for GMs, who can use it to style their strongholds and choose their allies and supporters. A villain's aesthetic might signal to heroes his or her terms of engagement and where he or she expects to fight. A villain's ideology can also be reflected in his or her style; it's a fun way to play with symbols in games.

- **Skulls:** These represent an overtly macabre sense of style. Anyone who decorates himself in dark colors, frightening images, and actual bones is shifted toward skulls.
- **Masks:** These are for villains who hide in plain sight or don't hide at all. Any character who is able to commit evil deeds under scrutiny is probably shifted toward masks.
- **Finery:** This is for a villain with elegant or grandiose tastes. He lives in castles, drinks fine wine, and tortures people to the sounds of opera.
- **Rags:** Rags are for a villain unconcerned with material goods beyond the tools that allow her to function.

Home Heraldry

Eventually some people begin to talk about your lack of a coat of arms. Others see heraldic coats of arms as an irritating fad that nobility from various regions impose on one another. However, there is information that can be communicated through a crest if you know how to use the symbols properly. A good crest can tell someone who has never met you the most essential parts of your life story.

Heraldic symbolism is a field of near infinite complexity. This will give you a basic understanding of the most common symbols.

✸ **Choose up to two colors:**

- O **Red:** courage, military prowess, strength
- O **Maroon:** endurance, triumph over adversity, patience
- O **Orange:** ambition, creativity, intellect
- O **Yellow:** hope, joy, peace
- O **Green:** prosperity, luck, reverence for nature
- O **Blue:** loyalty, honor, piety
- O **Purple:** magic, wisdom, curiosity, scholarship
- O **Silver:** wealth, mercantile achievement, pride in craftsmanship
- O **Gold:** royalty, divine power, righteousness
- O **Black:** prudence, diplomacy, political power

✸ **Choose up to three symbols from either category:**

ANIMALS

- O **Apex Predator:** This is used to convey strength, nobility, and courage. It is common for many noble houses to feature one excessively. Classically trained heraldic scholars take care to investigate a house displaying a predator, as the wheat must be separated from the chaff.

  Examples: lion, bear, tiger, owlbear, troll, predatory dinosaur, and umber hulk.

continued

- **Large Game:** This type of animal is used to convey endurance and heartiness. Larger game animals often appear on houses that hold harsh and unforgiving lands. There is also the suggestion of reverence for nature and a suggestion of a connection to druidic power.

  Examples: deer, elephant, rhinoceros, and leaf-eating dinosaur.

- **Beasts of Burden:** This generally suggests a connection to a background in production. Farming, milling, and even mining families that have risen to prominence often display a beast of burden to allude to the labor that brought them prosperity.

  Examples: ox, horse, golem, and animal skeletons.

- **Winged Predator:** Classically this is used to signify a connection to wisdom and justice. Houses affiliated with law enforcement often display raptors, but an explicit connection to law enforcement is not necessary. One just needs to value justice as a virtue to display a raptor.

  Examples: eagle, falcon, bat, griffin, and dragon.

- **Blessed Beast:** This suggests a connection to religious traditions. A family with prominent clerics and paladins typically bears a symbol of a creature connected to healing, rebirth, or duty.

  Examples: unicorn, phoenix, and angel.

- **Scavenger:** This type of creature became popular as mercantile families began to become politically prominent. Many noble houses saw rich merchants entering the political sphere as an affront to tradition. Some mercantile houses embraced that hostility and requested nontraditional animals be added to their crests. Today a scavenger represents canny negotiation, tenacity, and ambition.

  Examples: crow, rat, hyena, vulture, gelatinous cube, and goblin.

- **Sea Creature:** Heraldic traditions featuring symbols related to the sea could very well be an entire area of study. These symbols started appearing on the coats of arms of coastal noble houses and became extremely popular when wealthy maritime merchants were able to afford commission of their own crests. Families that worship ancient gods seem unable to resist alluding to their worship through symbols. Fish, crustaceans, cephalopods, and marine mammals have diverse and parallel meanings that rival the traditional land-based counterparts.

  Examples: fish, lobster, crab, squid, and starfish.

- **Undead/Aberration:** This suggests a connection to arcane studies and the mystic arts. It is often used by wizards, sorcerers, and magical theorists. Aberrant creatures are intimidating to those not schooled in heraldry, but seeing one on a crest simply means the family practices magic or values curiosity and scholarship.

  Examples: shoggoth, eye tyrant, skeleton, mind devourer, and aboleth.

- **Titan:** The oldest royal families and wealthiest merchant houses have worked tirelessly to distinguish themselves from what they see as imitators. In many places there are strict laws regarding which creatures are acceptable as heraldic symbols. Gaining the right to include a titan on a crest takes unimaginable political maneuvering, power, dazzling wealth, an ancient bloodline, or divine intervention. There are strict laws against adding a titan to a crest without permission. In many cases a titan crest is the most valuable thing a family owns, worth more than its land and armies.

  Examples: dragon, purple worm, and tarrasque.

OBJECTS

- **Swords:** The appearance of a sword is usually an allusion to military conquest and practice in warfare. Families with military officers, or that hold land won through bloody conquest, typically have a sword.
- **Shield:** This usually refers to the possession of a particularly impressive fortress or castle. This is seen as a subtler indicator of strength in land. It is not uncommon for a family that invests pride in a fortress or castle to simply add the silhouette of its property to the crest itself.
- **Mace:** This is an indicator of religious service or high station within a church. It is common for a mace to appear on the crest of a family that includes a well-known paladin. It is somewhat less common for this to occur if a family member is a cleric, but a mace can be found in both cases. A mace is almost always accompanied by a holy symbol or is held by an aspect of the deity the family worships.
- **Bow:** The crests of hunters, rangers, druids, and other wood-dwelling noble houses typically include a bow. It is a solid bet that a house flying a bow on its flag or crest will own large swaths of forested territory.
- **Hammer:** Mining and laborer families are traditionally fond of hammers. It used to be much easier to identify a mining linage, but many laborers have attained wealth and fame through adventuring and acknowledge the work of their ancestors by including a hammer in their crest.
- **Dagger:** This particularly threatening image is used by families that have built a reputation for shipping, trade, or transportation. Caravan drivers used to cut the hands off highwaymen and nail them, along with their weapons, to the sides of their carts to discourage ambushes. The first merchants to win the honor incorporated this grim warning into to their symbols. Families that made their fortunes though conducting trade in urban centers also use the dagger to warn rivals about the price for dealing in bad faith.

- **Compass/Gear/Clock:** Architects and engineers will often include a tool of their trade in their crest. Traditionally minded houses will choose easily recognizable tools, while newly wealthy engineering houses choose esoteric tools to distinguish themselves.

Create a Motto

The final step to creating a crest is the inclusion of a phrase that indicates the attitude or mission of your house. The meaning in these is usually fairly self-evident. However, an additional layer of meaning is hidden in the language a maxim is written in. Originally heraldic mottoes were simply written in a noble's native tongue. However, in the era of mercantile houses and wealthy adventurers, the appearance of language became something of a fashion statement. Some houses will feature a language that no one in the house has ever spoken fluently. Here are some of the most common languages that appear on crests and their meaning.

- **Dwarfish:** tradition, work ethic, trade.
- **Elvish:** beauty, royalty, reverence for nature.
- **Draconic:** ancient bloodline, arcane study, vast wealth.
- **Orcish:** military power, reverence for strength, tenacity.
- **Infernal:** reverence for law, diplomacy, reliability.
- **Celestial:** piety, royalty, honor.

"It Is My Distinct Pleasure to Announce…"

You have been invited to a royal gala. The page sent over to confirm your attendance bashfully informs you that the name you have provided is not sufficient, and they will require greater detail. Follow the prompts to craft a sprawling title befitting your accomplishments.

Name: Start with the most complete version of your name: first, last, middle, and any noble honorifics.

Job: Follow your name with your class or choose an esoteric way to phrase your class based on this chart.

Fighter Barbarian Ranger Rogue	O Sellsword O Soldier O Champion O Duelist	Wizard Sorcerer Warlock	O Mage O Arcanist O Veil Piercer O Thaumaturge
Bard Rogue	O Loremaster O Speaker O The Cunning O Thief	Druid Ranger	O Hunter O Guardian O Stalker O Verdant
Cleric Paladin	O Seer O Blessed of [Deity] O Saint O Crusader		

Origin: Where are you from? This can be your place of birth or a place you own land or a title.

 **Accomplishments:** This gives you a title based on your most impressive feats. Choose a title that sounds appealing in the left column and specify it using the right column.

○ Slayer ○ Scourge ○ Destroyer ○ Breaker ○ Toppler	Who is the most important man or beast you killed? What nation or army fell at your feet? What dark power was bested by your hand? Which dungeon did you plunder?
○ Champion ○ Master ○ Manipulator ○ Sage	What power do you have? What art do you teach? What is your style of combat? What element do you control?

○ Warden ○ Protector ○ Holder ○ Wielder ○ Touched	What famed weapon do you own?
	What is the name of a castle or stronghold you control?
	What is an artifact you control?
	What oath have you taken?
○ Knower ○ Namer ○ Guardian ○ Keeper ○ Unraveler	What is a secret you famously know?
	What god do you consort with?
	What far plane have you seen?
	What mystery have you revealed?

Ideology: Choose a title based on alignment. First select whether you would like to affirm or rebuke an ideology, then select an ideology.

Affirm	O Friend to O Seeker of O Ally of O Walker in	Rebuke	O Enemy to O Bane of O Scourge of O Opponent of
Good	O Light O Peace O Hope O Love	Evil	O Darkness O Horror O The Profane O The Forbidden
Law	O Order O Justice O Balance O Stability	Chaos	O The Gyre O Anarchy O Discord O Entropy

EXAMPLES

- Gwinnan Rockseeker, Crusader of the Grey Mountains, Breaker of the Elder Tomb, and Ally of Stability
- Iarrie Fairwind Thaumaturge of the Arsenio Halls, Knower of the Nine Words, and Walker in Light
- Rorlob Bloodletter, Sellsword of the Fallen Swamp, Master of Two Axes, and Seeker of Anarchy
- Prince Poros Silverthissel, Veil Piercer of the Thousand Wood, Sage of Shadows, and Scourge of Hope

God, No

As a living myth, you tend to attract attention from people in high places. Occasionally, this attention is disastrously unwanted. Using a d6, construct the tale of your hero hosting a troublesome deity as a houseguest.

Just as you are finishing preparations for a feast, you receive word that a prominent deity intends to attend by way of...

1. An angel who shines with cosmic light
2. A rat that speaks with the voice of a man
3. A prophecy written in a book bound in still-living flesh
4. A message written in the stars
5. Your bones vibrating with the rhythm of the unseen universe
6. All your potted plants simultaneously bursting into flames

The god is...

1. A quarrelsome war god with a reputation for starting fights
2. A capricious love god who seduces and discards lovers with thoughtless grace
3. A trickster who delights in engineering misfortune
4. A force of order who expects all things to move with precision
5. A lord of the underworld who reminds all who gaze upon him of mortality and woe
6. An elder thing that slithers on the edge of sanity, hungrily calling out to the mortal minds in ten thousand silent screams

Your feast is...

1. A rehearsal dinner for your friend's wedding
2. Your last chance to prove you can live a normal life
3. A fundraiser for a rival church
4. The one holiday when you get to relax and celebrate
5. An event that will be the subject of bard songs for decades
6. A date that *has* to go right

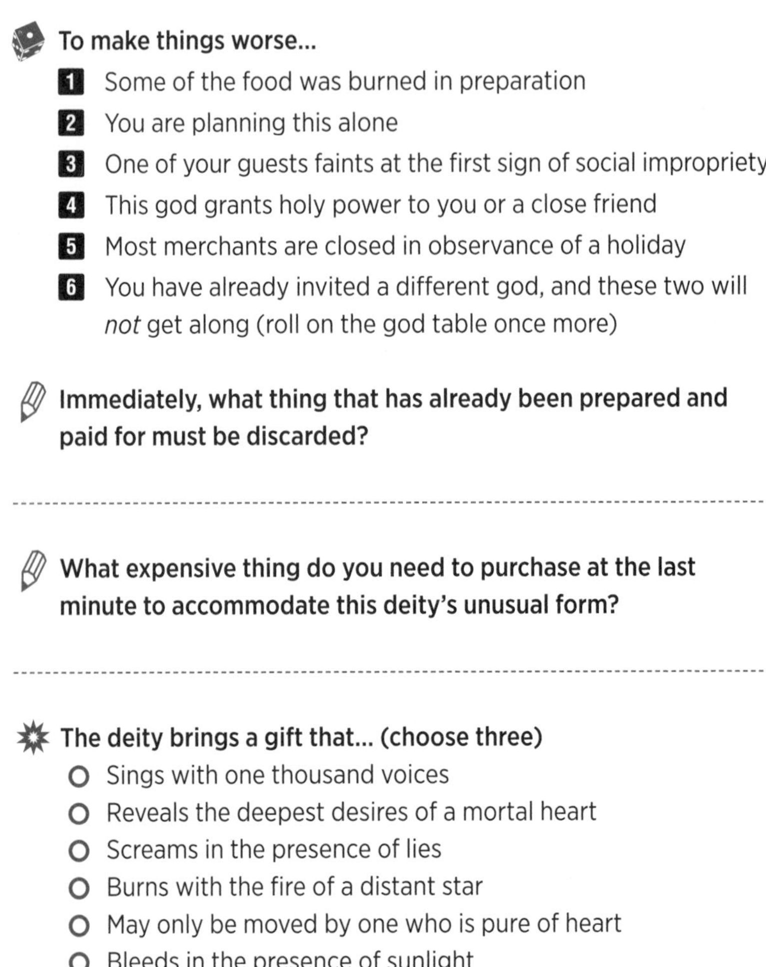

To make things worse...

1. Some of the food was burned in preparation
2. You are planning this alone
3. One of your guests faints at the first sign of social impropriety
4. This god grants holy power to you or a close friend
5. Most merchants are closed in observance of a holiday
6. You have already invited a different god, and these two will *not* get along (roll on the god table once more)

Immediately, what thing that has already been prepared and paid for must be discarded?

What expensive thing do you need to purchase at the last minute to accommodate this deity's unusual form?

The deity brings a gift that... (choose three)

- Sings with one thousand voices
- Reveals the deepest desires of a mortal heart
- Screams in the presence of lies
- Burns with the fire of a distant star
- May only be moved by one who is pure of heart
- Bleeds in the presence of sunlight
- Hums ominously
- Looks like a reproductive organ
- Makes people swap bodies when they touch it
- Heralds the end-times
- Smells like moss and rust
- Grants wishes at a terrible cost
- Activates seemingly unpredictably
- Can split mountains

The night progresses...

1. As one would expect
2. As the prophecy foretold
3. With the grim certainty of a funeral march
4. Despite an unwanted theological argument
5. Under the pretense of civil discussion
6. With sweet and easy conversation

By the end of the night, the god...

1. Excused himself with unexpected suddenness
2. Placed a curse on at least one guest
3. Repeatedly made desperate tearful apologies for fundamental inequalities that accompany mortal life
4. Transformed into an animal with the intent of seducing at least one guest
5. Fell asleep in your bed, impervious to mortal attempts at waking
6. Was still drinking, trying to keep things going

1. Die rolls as normal: this becomes a beloved annual tradition.
2. Die rolls off the table: you forget to properly store the leftovers, and they spoil.
3. Die rolls and the room is consumed in darkness: the god was most displeased.
4. The table spontaneously bursts into flames: the party was an unmitigated success.

Five Commandments

There are five rules observed by creatures in your service. They are the first lessons you teach and the foundation of any world shaped in your image. This helps you construct your character's vision for a future influenced by your will.

1. Always

This is the most important thing a person has to do to live by your ideals. If someone ever experiences doubt, he should be able to look to this to center himself.

Examples: Always...

- Ease suffering where you find it.
- Search for truth where it could be hidden.
- Trust your instincts to guide you.
- Focus yourself on serenity.
- Move before you set roots.

2. Never

The commandment is designed to prevent people from losing their way. It forbids an activity or way of thinking that you believe could lead them down a harmful path.

Examples: Never...

- Trust a person whose only achievement is wealth.
- Trade freedom for safety.
- Kill for something you cannot hold.
- Lie to a lover.
- Break an oath made with blood.

continued

3. Sacred

There is a place, concept, or thing that you believe holds divine importance. It should be something your followers are encouraged to seek out and protect.

✸ **Examples:**

- Freedom
- The forest
- Beer
- Music
- Sex

4. Sin

There is one crime you believe to be worse than all others. It is something your followers should work to remove from the world—something that would not be possible in a universe you controlled.

✸ **Examples:**

- Theft
- Dark magic
- Harming a child
- Killing in anger
- Selling out

5. Self

The final commandment is to define a follower's relationship with herself. If someone is to live by your example, how is she to treat herself?

✸ **Examples:**

- Sacrifice is the key to righteousness.
- Care for yourself so you may care for others.
- All for one, one for all.
- Heroes never run.
- There is no you before me.

Pocket Dimension

This is the weird, wonderful piece of creation to which your character escapes to be him- or herself. This exercise guides you to build a space tailored to an accomplished adventurer. Pick a style that suits you and then answer the prompts.

What style best suits you?

- O Opulent and indulgent
- O Natural and serene
- O Understated and homey
- O Otherworldly and surreal
- O Magical and whimsical
- O Utilitarian and spare
- O Beautiful and unique

Something to help you relax: This allows you to unwind with the weight of all your accomplishments and failures on your shoulders. It might be furniture, a form of entertainment, or even a recreational substance. It is either extremely rare and unusual or gallingly common.

Something to remind you of the past: This is generally something small that is given a place of honor. Looking at it might remind you of glory, happiness, or bittersweet regret. It can be anything, but it's best if it's something fragile.

Something to hold wisdom: Scrolls, books, maps, mystic orbs, and sacred totems—all of these contain wisdom. Even characters who are not gifted with exceptional wisdom or intelligence eventually acquire something they feel holds valuable information.

Something of immense wealth: It is almost impossible for you to spend years risking life and limb for shiny things without keeping something of value. Even if you place no value on gold and jewels, you've found something of beauty you appreciate.

A place to practice your skills: What good is having your own universe if it dulls the skills that helped you get it? How does this place help keep you sharp?

Something to help you hide secrets: Dark secrets have a way of finding brave adventurers. Some are too dangerous for the rest of the world to know. How do you keep them hidden away?

For the Myth That Has Everything

Your allies have the power to split mountains, part seas, and walk between raindrops. What gift could be worthy of them? Here's an exercise that prompts players to think of their companions and use that to craft items and gestures for them.

To restore what was sacrificed: In order to live with their choices, heroes often convince themselves that they are somehow different, that they don't have the needs of ordinary people. This gift reminds your friend that she is human. It should fulfill a need that your companion denies herself.

To give life to a memory: Sometimes good memories can be the only possessions a hero can call his own. This gift is a totem that brings sweet memories closer. It should be small, something your companion could easily afford but would never think to get himself.

---

continued

To demonstrate understanding: Being an adventurer means leaving the comforts of home and often passing through new worlds as a stranger. Returning to places that she once called home simply underscores the type of stranger a hero has become. This gift will show that someone knows and appreciates who she is. It should be personal and probably handmade.

To make an apology: Working together in life-and-death situations necessitates a strong professional relationship. Sometimes little offenses need to be swept away so the mission can succeed. This gift represents the apologies that were left unsaid. It should be something that sets aside pride and focuses on joy.

To restore wonder: Unraveling the mysteries of the unknown and facing the abyss every day creates a need to harden yourself against horror. Psychological self-defense can also limit access to joy grounded in awe. This gift embraces the strange and otherworldly beauty that both of you encounter day to day and opens your companion up to wonder. It should revolve around supernatural power and rare knowledge.

Inventory

Every veteran adventurer knows that traveling light is part of the job. Every adventurer also has their own reason for ignoring this advice. You have five items that you cannot bring yourself to part with, even though you know better.

Something rare: Even with years of adventuring experience, you have only seen something like this once. You know quite a bit about it, thanks to your particular areas of study; that knowledge tells you exactly how uncommon it is. It also tells you how useless it is to you for anything other than rarity for rarity's sake. There are probably better places for it than your bag, but the thought of never finding anything else like it stops you every time.

Something strange: You have seen a lot of weird and unexplainable stuff in your time. This particular curiosity was small enough to fit in your pack. In the many years you have had it in your possession, you have investigated it, though not vigorously. The shape, the material, the design—nothing about it makes sense. No one can tell you anything about it. It would be easier just to throw it away, but you can't.

Something circumstantially useful: You bought or found this object and instantly pictured a specific scenario in which it would come in handy. It is not an easy thing to come by, even with money and influence. You have had opportunities to make a profit by selling it, but you keep telling yourself you'll need it.

Something obsolete: You have grown past the need for this tool. You once depended on it to practice your trade, but the strength and power you have gained from years of heroism have made it completely unnecessary. All it does is take up space, but it reminds you of who you used to be, and that makes up for the extra weight.

Something unfinished: You have an object related to a quest you accepted long ago. This quest was always getting pushed aside so you could address more urgent matters. Out of a sense of honor or stubbornness, you never passed it on to someone else. Whatever obligation this was tied to has irretrievably failed, but discarding it would be admitting that failure. It causes you a pang of guilt every time you see it.

Art of Facts

Legends of your deeds have spread far and wide. Accompanying those tales are stories about the items you carry, which are myths in their own right. This exercise turns ordinary magic and mundane items into artifacts through guided exaggeration. Choose one of your items and roll to see how it changed in the eyes of people through rumor and stories.

Pick something you own:

- O A weapon
- O Armor
- O A cloak or cape
- O A book
- O A tool
- O A piece of jewelry
- O A building

What does it do?

What does it look like?

Exaggerations (roll a d6)

1. **Power:** People assume it is capable of feats well beyond its actual function based on twisted retellings of how you used it.
2. **Looks:** People describe it as looking far grander than it actually is, trying to make it appear as significant as they feel it is.

3 **History:** People say it shaped great events of the past. Often this results in natural phenomena or unrelated events being attributed to your possession.

4 **Origin:** People see the object as being otherworldly or miraculous in nature. They insist there were divine forces at work in its creation.

5 **Names:** People give it new names, which add a stylish personality to what is a simple tool.

6 **Superstition:** People attach portent and ritual to your possession to fit their exaggerated vision of your accomplishments.

Does the object have a name? ....

Would someone recognize it upon seeing it? ....

What does he or she expect it to look like? ....

What story is it famous for?

....

....

What problem would someone expect it to easily solve?

....

....

How would someone treat it if he or she found it?

....

....

Terror of Wisdom

A person as powerful as you has unraveled many of the world's secrets, sometimes without even trying. There are many who would do anything to learn what you know. They do not understand the unsettling consequences of revelation. Some knowledge is burdensome, and eats away at you in quiet moments.

Something common: You have learned that an ordinary household tool bears a resemblance to the agent of something sinister. What is it, and how can it be tested to ensure safety?

Something masked: There is an institution or group that ordinary folks accept as benign. However, you have discovered a fantastic purpose or origin for it. It might be harmless now, or it could still be an active conspiracy, but you know the hidden truth. What is it?

Something ubiquitous: Your journeys have taught you the true origin of something vast and ever present like the color of the sky or the shape of the moon. This truth has elements of the ancient origin myths but is most certainly different. What do you know? Does knowing it change the way you look at the world?

Something absurd: There is something that many view as miraculous, divine, or otherwise sacred. You have learned that its true nature is amusingly uninspired or insignificant. What is it? Has this knowledge caused you problems?

A Cutlass Carol

Three ghosts visit you to show you visions of the past, present, and future in hope of teaching you a lesson. The problem is the lesson isn't really worth learning.

One evening you return to your grand estate or stronghold after what you consider to be a long day.

 **As you begin to unwind, you are given a warning by an apparition... (roll a d6 to determine your visitor)**

1. Someone who was a party member for only a short time, as he died in an early dungeon
2. One of the first major enemies you vanquished
3. An animal companion or familiar you never clicked with
4. A mythical creature whose only job is issuing cryptic warnings and it is behind schedule
5. A mascot for a holiday you have never heard of
6. An angel who does not speak Common

After a confused back-and-forth, the messenger manages to inform you that on this night, you will be visited by three ghosts who will attempt to change your ways by showing you visions. You stare at the apparition with mild annoyance. It assures you this is very important and also unavoidable. You sigh and slump in your chair as the apparition disappears. After some minutes of fruitless waiting, you get up to tend to a chore just before the first ghost interrupts you.

The first spirit is... (roll a d6)

1. A childlike spirit of the past
2. A mascot for a defunct product
3. A screaming mass of teeth and tentacles
4. A sarcastic teen
5. The person who gave you your first kiss
6. A goblin who is preoccupied with stealing things

The spirit takes you into the past, but there is something off about what it is showing you: (choose two)

- O You are not part of the vision, and it is in no way related to you.
- O Everyone in the vision is asleep.
- O In the place you visit, it is too loud to understand what is going on.
- O You learn some trivial information that solves another problem unrelated to this whole situation.
- O The vision is presented with subtitles.

Once the vision ends, you try to protest to the spirit that there has been some kind of mistake, but you realize you are alone. Before you can collect your thoughts, the second spirit appears.

The second spirit is... (roll a d6)

1. A jovial bearded spirit of the present
2. Your least favorite party member
3. A sad gorilla
4. Bill Murray
5. Dracula
6. The god of loneliness

The spirit immediately takes you to a nearby bar. It spends the better part of an hour drinking with you and discussing your previous relationships. You feel as if you have found some closure on a few unresolved issues. However, you are still not entirely clear on why these visits are happening. As you are working through it, you feel the room grow cold and the shadows grow long as the final spirit arrives.

The final spirit is... (roll a d6)

1. Death
2. An extremely agitated-looking baboon that, seemingly at random, looks as if it will strike you before calming down
3. An extremely aged spirit of the new year
4. Santa Claus
5. A massive horse with a fiery mane
6. A large black dog with orange eyes

The spirit wordlessly beckons you into a void. Any protest you make is ignored. It takes you to the site of your future grave. It points wordlessly to the headstone as you demand some kind of meaning in this confused procession of ghosts. This moment lingers until you offer a response that pleases the spirit.

What do you say to convince the spirit that you have learned a lesson?

The next day you wake up in your bed, the memory of the spirits still fresh and vivid. What do you do? (choose one)

- O Order someone to buy you a goose, notorious enemy of the spirit realm.
- O Draft a lengthy letter of complaint to the deity you suspect was behind this bothersome event.
- O Heal as many injured children as you can find to get the spirits off your case.
- O Consult your cleric about your current regimen of potions.
- O Sell this estate as soon as possible, as it is clearly cursed.

84 Private Secrets

Create a mystery your character has left in her or his wake, one that adventurers and scholars will be pondering for years to come.

Your party broke or altered an artifact or a historical site. The truth is somewhat embarrassing; your party agreed to never discuss it. Historians have been left to fill in the gaps.

What really happened?

What's the most popular incorrect theory?

A group of people met through your party, and that loose association evolved into an organization with a notorious reputation.

What innocuous event brought them together?

What do they do?

What ominous name do outsiders call them?

An encounter with your party drastically altered the behavior of a well-known public figure.

Who was this person? --

How did he, she, or they change after encountering your group?

What is the wildest explanation you have heard for his or her change?

You quested after an object that turned out to be fake. Most scholars believe your group hid or destroyed it instead.

What was this object called? --

What did you find in its place? --

What do people think you did with it?

What danger is it supposed to represent?

It Sounds Good on Paper

Every great hero has to forge a relic; it's tradition. Being an experienced adventurer, you know that if you make something too useful, you'll end up with a team of adventurers breaking into your home to steal it.

Roll a d20 to determine the primary function of your artifact and see if you can come up with a secondary effect that would ward off unwanted intruders.

1. Turns lead into gold
2. Grants eternal life
3. Grants wishes
4. Can imprison a powerful soul
5. Allows the user to see people as they really are
6. Cures any ailment
7. Reshapes mountains
8. Returns to its original shape, no matter how it is damaged
9. Answers any question
10. Navigates by the stars
11. Travels between realities
12. Controls the flow of time
13. Swaps the bodies of two creatures
14. Allows its owner to freely speak with the dead
15. Grants the power of a god
16. Makes the user invulnerable
17. Erases the wicked deeds of whoever uses it
18. Allows someone to experience his or her past anew
19. Can kill an immortal being
20. Allows omnipotent control over a separate dimension

Given the function of your creation, what would make someone think twice about stealing it but not totally rob it of value?

I Knew Them Well

Pick a mythic figure or deity in the setting and answer the prompts to discover your personal connection to him, her, or them.

What miraculous power does he use without thought or ceremony?

To the world his power is awe inspiring, but he treats it like a part of himself that is no more remarkable than a limb. What miracle have you witnessed this being perform?

What does he always take his time doing?

Some picture beings with miraculous powers always using them to make every problem simple and easy. There is something your friend always takes care to do the long way. What is it, and why does he choose to invest his time in it?

What mundane thing gives him satisfaction?

In order to meet a legend, you have to be in the same place. What thing that most people find quite ordinary draws a person like your friend to the material plane?

What is his most prominent emotional quality?

Too many gods and myths are famous for wrath or wisdom, but to you your friend is someone with a nuanced emotional life. What is he like in your experience?

What small secret did he confide in you?

Most information about legendary figures is based on conjecture and exaggeration. You were given real information firsthand. What truth lies behind a common story?

What always gives him difficulty? It can be a great puzzle, an unfinished labor, or a simple thing many mortals accept as a normal part of life, but something is always difficult for your friend to understand or do. He tries nonetheless.

How did you first meet?

Why do you believe he was interested in you?

Alive Only in Memory

You know of a place that no longer exists. It is a part of you that you carry with you everywhere, but it no longer has a home in your world. Answer the prompts to develop a sense of this place and what it means to you.

Why do you care about this place? (choose one)

- O I helped build it.
- O It saved me.
- O It almost destroyed me.
- O It helped make me what I am.

What destroyed this place? (choose one)

- O Disaster
- O Entropy
- O Hubris
- O Invasion
- O Corruption

When you visit the site where it used to be, what do you see?

- O Empty ruins
- O Something wholly unfamiliar and alien
- O A hollow shell where the place you knew once stood
- O A monument to what once was

When you close your eyes there, what feeling do you get?

What was the most distinctive physical feature of this place?

What broken part of that feature still remains?

Who was your most trusted friend in this place?

Is that friend still alive?

What was the biggest change in your relationship after you left?

Did you watch this place collapse?

What spared you the destruction it suffered?

What do you miss most about it?

What unintentional tribute have you made to it?

Collecting Dust

In your home you have objects on your mantel that many believe are lost to time, that some would be shocked to learn exist at all. What are these things, and how do you treat them?

Something Dangerous

This is the sort of object that creatures obsessed with darkness make it their life's work to obtain. In the wrong hands it is capable of causing untold destruction and suffering. It seeks victims and enablers to wreak havoc. In your hands it is harmless.

What does it look like?

When did you acquire it?

When did it give up on tempting you?

Something Ancient

This is something almost as old as life itself. If it hadn't been with you, this object would have crumbled to dust long ago.

Why do you think this artifact is worth preserving?

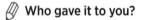

Where do you keep it?

How much do you know about it?

Something Beautiful

This is a labor of profound love and grace or the product of the majesty of nature. It can be unique or common, but its beauty is undeniable.

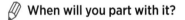

How often do you appreciate this object?

Who gave it to you?

When will you part with it?

Sign of a Legend 89

There is a symbol or mark that has become associated with your name. This exercise tells you what it is, where it appears, and its relationship to the world. Answer the prompts to create your symbol.

Your symbol is... (choose one)

- O Something that can be carved with a blade
- O A physical object that can be left behind
- O Something complex made with magic
- O The general chaotic state of the place you left behind
- O An appropriated recognizable symbol or crest
- O Something laid in the dirt

What does it look like?

What is your intent when leaving this symbol behind?

In what situations do you leave it?

What type of person usually finds this symbol?

Who reacts positively to this symbol? ------------------------------

Who reacts negatively to this symbol? ------------------------------

What superstition has formed about it?

----

90 Hobby

In addition to the skills you picked up as a heroic adventurer, you also mastered a mundane craft and honed it to legendary perfection. This will tell you what that is and what impact it had on yourself and the world.

My hobby... (choose one)

- O Uses my hands
- O Challenges my mind
- O Expresses my emotions
- O Demands creativity
- O Takes patience
- O Exercises care
- O Calms my nerves
- O Replaces a lost joy

I... (choose one)

- O Have mastered it just as I mastered all things
- O Seek to understand it
- O Enjoy the feeling of struggling
- O Am hopelessly untalented in this area

What new skill have you chosen to learn?

Who first taught you this?

What about it brings you peace?

Whom has this hobby made you admire?

What do you do with the products of your labor?

Five Lives 91

Your deeds have touched five individuals. Answer the prompts to make your legend richer.

The Aided

You showed this person a relatively small kindness that radically changed her life. You may never have discovered the full extent of what you did for her, but she can never forget.

What favor did you do for her?

What did you think of this gesture in the moment?

What does she tell people about it today?

The Liberated

You rescued an individual or group from a desperate situation. It could have been imprisonment, servitude, or a weighty obligation.

How much did you sacrifice to win his freedom?

What kind of gratitude did he show you?

How has his freedom helped others?

The Empowered

You have helped someone become strong or skillful. She was able to use this strength to drastically change her life.

What made you want to teach her?

Why did she want to learn from you?

Are you proud of what she has become?

The Redeemed

You prevented someone from walking a dark path that could have ended with a great deal of pain and suffering. Your intervention also set them toward a path of righteousness.

What prompted you to get involved with this person's life?

How intimate was the process of reforming them?

What do they think of you now?

The Humiliated

Perhaps with the intention of teaching a lesson or righting a wrong, you overpowered and humiliated someone. Her reputation drastically changed after that incident.

What was she like before?

How did people discover the news of her defeat?

What is her life like now?

---

92 You Made It Weird

The chimera, the owlbear, and the gibbering mouther: beloved monsters created by powerful beings in a bizarre competition. This exercise will help you take an existing monster and make it into something strange. Roll on tables and answer the questions to create a memorable abomination.

Roll a d20 to pick an animal or monster to start with:

1. Bear
2. Tiger
3. Eagle
4. Horse
5. Wolf
6. Deer
7. Crocodile
8. Snake
9. Shark
10. Spider
11. Octopus
12. Turtle
13. Human
14. Vampire
15. Dragon
16. Troll
17. Ghost
18. Golem
19. Mimic
20. Skeleton

Once you have your base creature, choose three of the following tables and roll a d6 to find qualities that will change it. You can also roll the d20 a second time to combine your base creature with another creature. Think of a way the new qualities will change the way the creature looks and behaves.

Class	Abilities
1 Mammal	1 Acute sense of smell
2 Avian	2 Camouflage
3 Reptile	3 Echolocation
4 Fish	4 Metamorphosis
5 Crustacean	5 Electromagnetic senses
6 Ooze	6 Intelligence

Body Parts	Elements
1 Eyes	1 Fire
2 Legs	2 Air
3 Tail	3 Water
4 Mouth	4 Earth
5 Tentacles	5 Time
6 Horns	6 Magic

Aggression Instinct

1. **Ambush predation:** It waits for prey in order to strike.
2. **Territorial:** It protects a particular place.
3. **Pursuit predation:** It talks to and stalks its prey over distances.
4. **Multiplication:** It requires violence to reproduce.
5. **Hoarding:** It seeks to collect and save different objects and protects them from intruders at all costs.
6. **Constant:** This creature is ceaselessly aggressive as long as it's awake.

Defenses

1. **Regeneration:** It heals rapidly from most injuries.
2. **Shell:** It has a thick protective outer layer.
3. **Poison:** It is toxic for most beings to come in contact with it.
4. **Spikes:** This creature has barbs or quills.
5. **Elemental resistance:** It is resistant to certain elemental attacks.
6. **Insubstantial:** Many attacks will pass through its body harmlessly.

What does it look like now?

In what situation is it most dangerous?

What is most comical or strange about it?

In the Eyes of Mortals 93

Since you're a living legend, people are interested in your movements. When you pass through a town, dozens of stories pop up with varying degrees of accuracy. Part of that comes from people twisting stories, but the root is based on the details different people notice. Use the prompts to consider what a stranger might see when she, he, or they looks at you.

A Watchman

Tasked with maintaining peace and safety, a watchman must be skilled at identifying someone who poses a threat. Truly gifted watchmen have to know who is beyond their ability to police with force.

When someone eyes you with suspicion, what does he find?

A Tavern Server

Servers survive by judging who can tip and what they need to do to charm a profit.

What does a person see when she watches you drink and feast?

A Pickpocket

Pickpockets want money and to avoid getting caught.

Are your wealth and power obvious to someone assessing you as a target?

A King or Queen

Those with royal blood are accustomed to subservience and to thinking in terms of the good of the state.

When someone born with power looks in your eyes, do they find a threat, a resource, or something else?

A Child

Children are learning about their world, protecting a delicate interpretation of reality. They are open to noticing impossible details that adults dismiss.

What does a person who embraces the impossible see in you?

Hangover

You lost a powerful artifact at some point last night. Retrace your steps to reclaim what is yours. Many things are possible about last night, but since you were drunk, you don't remember any of them. Perhaps you met a being akin to a god, you visited another plane, you destroyed something extraordinary, or your lost item drastically changed something while it was gone.

You wake up... (roll a d6)

1. In the bed of an enemy or rival
2. In a lavishly decorated room that has been utterly trashed
3. Surrounded by fallen foes
4. In a jail cell surrounded by guards
5. In a pocket dimension very unlike your reality
6. On the back of a galloping creature

After checking your possessions you find that you are missing an immensely important artifact. This is extremely distressing because... (choose two)

- ○ It was entrusted to you by a dear friend
- ○ It is needed for a monumentally important ceremony
- ○ It has the potential to destroy the world
- ○ You will die without it
- ○ You will have need of it very soon

You notice that you have an unexpected companion. This person... (roll a d6)

1. Treats you as if you have a totally different personality
2. Keeps alluding to a fight that happened last night
3. Refuses to leave you alone, insisting you owe him or her something
4. Is apparently now married to you
5. Speaks to you as though you have been friends for years
6. Does not speak a language you understand

Retracing your steps brings you to an unsavory corner of the universe: the sort of place most people avoid at all costs. You don't remember being here, but the creatures who frequent this place eye you with a sense of familiarity. What is this place?

What does it look like? --

Who is in charge here? --

After talking to someone who had a clearer idea of what happened to you last night than you did, you discover what happened to the artifact. The only way to get it back will be... (roll a d6)

1. Making an uncomfortable apology
2. Winning a large contest
3. Performing an elaborate heist
4. Confronting an old enemy
5. Assuming a false identity
6. Traveling through time

How does your new companion help prepare you for this task?

Roll a d6 to see how your attempt to reclaim what was lost goes:

1. It is destroyed in your attempt to reclaim it.
2. The person you'd least like to know what you did discovers it.
3. The artifact ends up in more trustworthy hands than yours.
4. You reclaim the artifact, but it is permanently changed.
5. You reclaim the artifact, but you are nearly killed in the process.
6. You reclaim the artifact, and it is as if nothing ever happened.

As you and the collection of creatures you met on this adventure share a drink, what do you feel you have learned?

Apprentice 95

Heroes who reach a certain level of mastery often want to pass on some of their knowledge. Others find that they are inundated with offers from potential students whether they want them or not. Dream as you might, there is no such thing as a perfect student.

✸ **Select the qualities of your apprentice, ensuring he, she, or they have at least one A, B, C, D, and E.**

TALENT

- O **A.** You have never met a person as gifted as your student. She understands something intuitively that you grappled with for years. With careful instruction she could change the world.
- O **B.** He takes in new information with easy grace and understanding. Even difficult lessons are mastered within a short amount of time.
- O **C.** Like any journeyman in your field, they demonstrate moments of brilliance and others of inscrutable foolishness.
- O **D.** This student has no natural knack for this sort of work. Left to his own devices, he would never reach any level of mastery.
- O **E.** You have never met anyone who struggles with basic principles as much as this student does. Any other master would have written her off as hopeless long ago.

continued

EGO

- O **A.** This student possesses an almost supernatural humility. They do not revel in success or status. Their only desire is learning.
- O **B.** She is a generous and loving soul. It is incredibly rare to catch her in a moment of self-satisfaction, and when you do, it is more charming than worrisome.
- O **C.** You have to walk a careful line of praise and criticism to keep him in the best condition to learn. Like most people he could walk many paths given the proper treatment.
- O **D.** They are a victim of crippling self-doubt. They are not confident even in areas in which she is truly gifted.
- O **E.** He is easily the most arrogant creature you have ever met. He could be a danger to himself and even the world if left unchecked.

RELIABILITY

- O **A.** She is consistent and trustworthy. You'd feel comfortable entrusting her with monumental responsibility that even you could not shoulder.
- O **B.** There is almost no task you would hesitate to give this student. However, you can allow your trust to go only so far. The darkest secrets must be kept safe.
- O **C.** When directed carefully they are capable of a great deal. Without that direction they could easily find trouble. Perhaps they will grow in time.
- O **D.** She requires almost constant attention to accomplish even simple things. You are careful to keep even simple temptations away from her.
- O **E.** This person is a walking disaster. Without care and attention he will find a way to create catastrophe out of even simple situations.

STUDIOUSNESS

- **A.** Her dedication is awe inspiring. She constantly pulls off miraculous feats of academic dedication.
- **B.** He is feverishly committed to study, often at risk of personal health and safety. It's mostly good, but it can get out of hand without your intervention.
- **C.** While some areas of your craft capture her attention easily, you work hard to keep her focused on the complete scope of her studies.
- **D.** They don't seem to be interested in most of what you have to teach. You often have to trick or mislead them in order to get lessons across.
- **E.** This is the most insufferably lazy person you have ever met. She does not seem to understand that one has to work in order to learn.

MORALITY

- **A.** This is a living saint. He is not tempted by even minor vices and has a patience and love for other living things that is truly beautiful.
- **B.** This is a good and righteous person with few flaws. You do worry that, presented with the wrong circumstances, it is possible that could change.
- **C.** They carry vice and prejudice like many who are born into an imperfect world.
- **D.** He is a dishonorable, reprehensible lowlife. Many would call him a monster, and perhaps he will become one.
- **E.** You have never met a more terrifying individual in your life. She is relentlessly and carefully dedicated to wickedness. Perhaps even you do not know her true nature.

96 Five Enemies

Take a look at some of the foes you have faced in your past. Answer the prompts to construct a rogues' gallery for yourself.

The Fools

This is a small group of recurring enemies whom you have encountered more than once in your travels. They are not a serious threat, but they do tend to get in the way.

What do they call themselves?

What is their most prominent flaw?

Why do you never deal with them using lethal force?

The Rival

This is someone you have faced many times who is not always an enemy.

What is his greatest skill?

What asset does he possess that you do not?

What makes you respect him?

The Authority

This is a powerful organization or nation. It has far-reaching influence and many allies. This makes it almost impossible to face it directly.

What is its most frightening aspect?

What do you most detest about its ideology?

How do you usually recognize its handiwork?

The Leviathan

This is a bestial foe of inconceivable power. It threatens large-scale destruction.

What is the most effective way to keep what you care about safe from it?

Why is it never simple to confront?

What historical cataclysm do you attribute to it?

---

continued

The Nemesis

This is a powerful and calculating foe more dangerous to you than any other. Perhaps you did not start out as important to each other, but after repeated confrontations you bear a mutual disdain for each other.

What is the most devastating blow she has dealt you?

What is the most humiliating defeat she suffered at your hands?

Why must you thwart her at any cost?

Impossible Trial

You are inundated with requests from potential students clearly unworthy of your knowledge. To dissuade students you have no interest in dealing with, you have crafted three impossible tasks an apprentice must complete before working with you. Answer the prompts to create these labors and explain how they are eventually completed.

Power

The first challenge is something you believe is physically impossible. It may be moving an immense object, conquering a natural obstacle, or enduring a taxing hardship.

What do you ask of people?

How does a clever apprentice circumvent the danger of this challenge?

Possession

The next task is to capture something impossible to possess, like an incorporeal being or abstract concept.

What thing do you ask for, and how do you request it be delivered?

What resource allows the right apprentices to bring you what you believed you would never hold?

Competition

The final challenge is to best you in a competition that you know you would never lose. It should be something you have unquestionably mastered.

What do you choose, knowing you will never be beaten?

What moment during this competition convinces you to let them win?

Not Looking to Get Merlined

Taking on an apprentice can be a life-changing event. Some masters gain new knowledge, personal fulfillment, and a meaningful relationship. Others get sealed in a tree.

✸ **This is a list of actions taken by your apprentice. If you find an action suspicious, check its box. At the end of the exercise determine whether you trust your apprentice or not and roll a d100 to find out what happens.**

- ○ You are approached by a young person who wishes to become your apprentice.
- ○ Almost immediately, she impresses you with her skill and knowledge.
- ○ She is undeniably attractive.
- ○ She is eager to help with even unpleasant tasks in your routine.
- ○ Her enthusiasm makes you feel a little guilty tasking her with difficult chores.
- ○ She shows talent and progresses quickly through basic lessons.
- ○ She asks questions about your abilities and techniques that just about anyone could have heard about through stories.
- ○ She follows those questions with insightful follow-ups that demonstrate a keen understanding of the subject.
- ○ Her line of questioning begins to flirt with forbidden/privileged information without actually crossing the line.
- ○ She reacts with apology and surprise when you turn the conversation away from dangerous topics.
- ○ She becomes an undeniable asset to your work.
- ○ You sneer at the thought of doing things that were so much more difficult before you took on your apprentice.
- ○ You find her diligently studying an advanced technique you did not personally teach her.
- ○ She reacts with surprise when she discovers you were watching.
- ○ She reacts with disappointment when you insist she keep to your prescribed syllabus.

- She risks her life to protect something precious to you.
- She is seriously wounded in the process.
- She apologizes profusely for what almost happened.
- You spend long weeks nursing her back to health.
- In that time it becomes clear her dreams and ambitions are quite close to your own.
- What attracted you to her initially is underscored by her passion and dedication to ideas you hold sacred.
- She thanks you for your care with tearful earnestness.
- She has the most captivating eyes you have ever seen.
- She resumes her studies with commendable diligence to make up for lost time.
- You notice a change in her demeanor. She has difficulty focusing on certain tasks and has trouble meeting your eyes.
- After an emotional and difficult day of training, you confront her about her behavior.
- She tries to object and becomes flustered.
- She confesses she has fallen in love with you.
- You cannot deny that some part of you returns these feelings.
- Life returns to a better sort of normal, and you are able to share secrets with an easy trust.
- Both of you reach new levels of understanding as masters of your craft and as people.
- You feel comfortable sharing forbidden knowledge that you would not trust another soul with.
- She takes in the information with solemn dedication.
- She plans a romantic outing in the forest.
- You arrive to find a picnic set up under a tree—a very large tree.
- There is a note that reads, "I will join you soon, my love. Please sit and enjoy yourself while you wait for me."
- The basket is unopened and calls to you ominously.
- The day is gentle and sweet, the ideal conditions for passion.
- You hear soft footsteps from the other side of the tree.

continued

Add the number of boxes you checked and multiply by five. That number is your Suspicion. Decide in this moment if you trust your apprentice. Roll a d100 and determine what happens based on your trust or distrust.

Trust	Distrust
Rolled under your Suspicion You missed key red flags that bards will name as they sing of your folly years from now. If it's any consolation, you are unlikely to hear those songs from inside this tree.	**Rolled under your Suspicion** You cleverly thwart an attempt to imprison you. You also managed to obscure key truths throughout your apprentice's training, making her mostly harmless—at least to you.
Rolled over your Suspicion Your apprentice has always been worthy of your love and trust. The basket contains a ring that she will use to pledge her love to you.	**Rolled over your Suspicion** Your apprentice has always been worthy of your love and trust. Unfortunately, on this day you betray her out of fear. Something beautiful is forever lost to you.

99 Crisis of Faith

Faith works differently in a world where gods routinely grant miraculous power, speak to their followers, and occasionally appear in the mortal realm. Believers do not struggle with questions of a god's existence but rather its intentions and ideology. These questions will challenge your relationship with a deity.

What deity have you worshipped or allied yourself with?

What has it done that you considered harsh or cruel?

If you were in that position, could you do such a thing?

In what tragic event did the deity choose not to intervene?

What would you have done with its divine power?

When have you seen the deity exhibit an otherworldly perspective?

What have you sacrificed in your god's name?

Do you trust your god?

Do you believe in it?

Why or why not?

100 Your Kind of King

Your life of adventuring has ended with you sitting on the throne. A hero becoming a ruler is always a unique story. Use this exercise to see what kind of ruler you have become.

- **Attitude:** Everyone approaches the throne differently. One's attitude toward royal duty does not dictate the quality of one's rule, but it does change the experience of leadership.
  - ○ **Traditional:** You are fond of custom and propriety. You uphold the traditions of the beings who preceded you and maintain a sense of order.
  - ○ **Revolutionary:** You believe in change and novelty. You are fine doing away with traditional strictures if you feel they do not suit your vision for your kingdom.
  - ○ **Sworn:** You approach your responsibilities with solemn reverence. You see your position as a tremendous and humbling responsibility.
  - ○ **Afflicted:** You see this position as a necessary evil or perhaps even an impediment to your true aims. You try to avoid the nuisance of this role whenever you can.

- **Action:** Leaders are defined by their deeds. There are, however, innumerable ways of approaching the same problem.
  - ○ **Diplomatic:** You look to negotiate first, solving problems and gaining resources by making allies and cutting deals.
  - ○ **Strategic:** You take a proactive approach to problem-solving. You capture resources and control forces like moving pieces on a chessboard.
  - ○ **Delegated:** You rely on a network of skilled agents to carry out your commands. You always have the perfect person for a job, whether that's negotiating a treaty or leading an army.
  - ○ **Personal:** You take on challenges on your own when you can. You lead the charge in battle and personally represent your kingdom at any table.

continued

- **Style:** The way a kingdom and its ruler look can say a lot about both.
  - **Egotistical:** The style of the kingdom is modeled to celebrate you, the ruler. Banners, monuments, and places of political import leave no question who is in charge.
  - **Nationalistic:** You are decorated to celebrate the place and culture you represent.
  - **Opulent:** The throne room and any important civic structures are built to celebrate the cultural and artistic achievements of your kingdom.
  - **Militaristic:** The throne room and any important civic structures are built to celebrate the power of you as the ruler and the military that protects the kingdom.

About the Author

James D'Amato is the creator and game master of the *One Shot* podcast, as well as several spin-off podcasts dedicated to RPG gameplay. He trained at Second City and iO in Chicago in the art of improvisational comedy. He now uses that education to introduce new people to role-playing and incorporates improvisational storytelling techniques to create compelling and entertaining stories for RPG campaigns and one-shot adventures.